EVERYDAY SOUL DANCES

EVERYDAY SOUL DANCES

A Guide to Soulful Living in the Midst of Uncertain Times

Elaine Hoem

BALBOA.PRESS
A DIVISION OF HAY HOUSE

Balboa Press books may be ordered through booksellers or by contacting:

Balboa Press
A Division of Hay House
1663 Liberty Drive
Bloomington, IN 47403
www.balboapress.com
844-682-1282

Print information available on the last page.

ISBN: 978-1-9822-3359-4 (sc)
ISBN: 978-1-9822-3358-7 (hc)
ISBN: 978-1-9822-3357-0 (e)

Library of Congress Control Number: 2019913534

Balboa Press rev. date: 04/04/2023

DEDICATION

To the Divine Mother who lives within us all

To the Spiritual Teachers
Who show the way

To Don, Bob, and Keith
My teachers, my gifts, my sons

PREFACE

I never intended to write a book. I had a fulfilling career as a psychotherapist and lived an idyllic and serene life at Lake Tahoe. I taught meditation classes and led women's retreats. Over many years, I was drawn to spiritual exploration and the development of soulful ways of being. Living at Lake Tahoe had fulfilled an old dream. My life felt complete.

Several years ago, however, I heard a clear inner voice that I was to write a book. I even was given the name. It was to be called "Everyday Soul Dances." I now know that this voice was that of the Divine Feminine. Her voice has been with me at various times since then. The next message, some months later, was the longer text that you will find as Her first message in this book. I became a scribe as Her words danced through me onto the first pages. You will also find Her poems within these pages.

One of my names for Her, for this sacred energy, for the feminine face of God, is Goddess. You may find that you prefer to use other names that are more familiar to you. As you read these words, please use those names that are most evocative for you.

When we engage in spiritual practices, we are uniting with the Divine. These moments become our unique soul dance. Your Everyday Soul Dances will illumine the way to align with spirit, with your highest possible Self. And you will be guided in every step.

Over the years of writing this book, I found that I was able to add words of my own to Her's. Yet always there were the essential questions at the forefront of my mind. "What does it take to become conscious?" And "What does it mean to become an *Everyday Soul Dancer*?" Along the way, in pursuit of this writing, I was called to look more deeply into my soul and contemplate all that I found there. As a result, I became even more dedicated to the paths written about here. I found myself growing in awareness of what a large and vital part the Divine Feminine plays in all our lives, no matter how we identify our gender. All we need to do is invite Her in. Once I did, I became more centered in my Self and my place in the world. My life became more graceful. Now, I am even more excited to share these ways with you. May you enjoy and benefit from your journey as an Everyday Soul Dancer.

Namaste

DISCLAIMER

The ways of this book are guides into your inner world. There may be times in which the contemplations and meditations open unexplored parts of your psyche that are unexpected and could cause confusion, fear, or a revisiting of past trauma. If such experiences happen in your explorations of these words and you have any difficulty calmly integrating them, please schedule some time with a psychotherapist who has a familiarity with the spiritual journey and who can help you heal whatever challenges you are facing. This is important to do to become free of blockages and old karmic impressions that you are meant to release during this lifetime. The resultant freedom will be well worth such exploration and healing.

FOREWORD

I have known Elaine for 40 years as a friend and a colleague. Her book EVERYDAY SOUL DANCES is a culmination of her work as a therapist and her spiritual journey over all these years. It is a fascinating read, written with such grace, kindness, and love. It is a wonderful invitation to the reader to embark on an incredible journey. As I read it, I felt Elaine was speaking directly to me in a very personal way. I expect other readers will have similar experiences.

This book comes at a perfect time given the current ways of our world. It shines a light for readers to discover many other ways of experiencing life: ways filled with hopefulness and love, ways to hold high states amid stressful times.

Please read this book and practice Elaine's suggested ways. You may be surprised to find that you grow in loving, in strength of being, and spiritual connectedness. As a result, you may find your world becoming more expansive, enriched in relationships and beauty.

Enjoy your journey with EVERYDAY SOUL DANCES.

Patti Davin, Ph.D. M.F.T.

CONTENTS

NAMASTE

I honor the place in you.
In which the entire universe dwells.
It is a place of love, of light.
Of truth and peace.
When you are in that place in you
And I am in that place in me.
We are one.

PART I

RETURNING HOME TO YOURSELF

CHAPTER 1

LISTEN TO THE WORDS OF THE MOTHER

My Most Beautiful Dear One,

I am She who is known throughout time and by all people and by many names. I AM. I am the Divine Mother who resides within us all. I am Mother Mary. I am Shekinah, Diana, Sophia, Tara, Quan Yin, Grandmother Spider Woman, Ixchel, and the Devi. I am Kali. I am Durga and the Goddess Kundalini Shakti. Some know Me as The Most Compassionate One and others as the Healer of the World. I am the one who gives birth to all of creation. All of life flows from Me and through Me.

As you read these words, call Me by the names that please you most. I will answer. I invite you to come to Me so that you may discover the myriad beautiful possibilities within yourself. You are an integral part of Me, and you are vital in bringing balance and peace to the ways of what is happening in our world today.

I call you My Beloved.

Let me tell you a story so that you can remember who I Am and who you truly are.

I am your inner Self, and I Am All That Is. My presence in your life is full and radiant once you open to our Oneness and our communion. I come in the feminine form at this time to help rebalance the energies of the inner feminine and the inner masculine, the dark and the light, the good and the evil so that more harmonious ways of living can be manifest within each person and the collective throughout this world. In this way, I welcome all beings.

Through Me, all is formed, and unto Me, everything returns. There is nothing separate from Me. I Am the light, and I Am the way. My

1

energies have formed the sun, the moon, and all the stars in the heavens. I Am the fiery core of the earth. The energies of My divine consciousness flow in all the waters of our world. The mountains contain My majesty and My strength. You will find Me in the most exquisite snowflake and the brilliance and fragrance of your favorite rose. My ways are infinite, formed from love, and supremely free and flowing.

These same energies create and enliven the cells within your body. I Am both that which is and that which is not. I Am in your first breath and your dying breath. I Am a guide for worn ways of living that you will release, and I Am in that for which you strive. In all ways, I Am a touchstone for you to return home to your most sacred Self.

I want you to know Me in the faces of nature and the myriad forms of beauty and abundance, sorrow, and longing, and even in the fierce patterns of creation and destruction. You will find Me in your strengths, your visions, in your brokenness, and in your awe. I Am in the flow of your tears, in your most imaginative expressions and most loving ways. My energies are astonishing powers teeming within and throughout. It is My energies that fill you with vibrancy and vitality. I express within you and through you eternally.

In this union, we are One. I call to you. When you seek to know Me, I Am the One who answers. I help you heal, and it is My love that flows through the ways of your loving of others.

I am here to invite you on a journey—a pilgrimage into the heart of soulful matters, and a calling to turn within. It is here that you will find that which is sacred within you. It is with Me that you will deepen your love and awaken your wisdom. It is here that you will bow in reverence to All That Is.

I am the one energy that has manifested and is manifesting everything that has ever been created for all times. This energy is both astonishing and barely conceivable by the human mind. And you, Dear One, are an essential expression of this energy of I AM.

Think of it this way. I Am the macrocosm, and you are the microcosm made of the same substances of all the delicate and fierce energies of which the universe is formed. I Am the creator and the container of it all. You are a precious and unique manifestation of this great, primordial, and unfathomable consciousness reaching through all of life. Each person and *each creation is extraordinary, of great value, and worthy of the honor in which you always are held.*

This world is flush with richness, abundance, and wonder. You are a vital part of this divine and universal design. I see you as magnificent! You see, you are My creation. I express through you. And, always, if you call, I will bring you home to Me.

This is the story of your journey back home to your highest Self. You will find Me in the depths of your soul, in the quiet of your reflections, in the pleasures of your play, and in life experiences born of sacred ways of living. You will know Me when you pay graceful attention to daily tasks. You will know Me when you move from ego and judgment into all-embracing and loving ways.

You will find Me when you access your strengths, in your dreams, and your sorrows. I am calling to you in many ways and through myriad forms. My call is unique to each person. As you learn to know Me in all your ways, you will access sacred energies to expand and magnify your life and the lives of those around you. Your role is to know Who I Am within the sacredness of your body and from there, out into the farthest reaches of the cosmos. Whenever you ask, I Am present to you. I Am always present in all forms of love.

Your soul knows the larger story of your life. Open and be in awe. Have your eyes open soft and wide to see beyond what you see in your ordinary days. Allow your mind to be as spacious and as clear as a cloudless sky. As you enter the realms of your soul's dances, you will find new wonders, new beginnings, and new ways to celebrate each day. Think of your spiritual journey as lights in the harbor of your soul's passage leading the way, to your rightful home.

With attention, awareness, and focus, you will release all that comes from wounding, suffering, and lesser sacred ways so that you can fully embrace that which is expansive. You are entering a path of liberation and exquisite freedom. In these pages, I invite you to return home to the knowing and honoring of all parts of yourself as you interface with universal ways, deepening knowledge and more exquisite loving. Within these pages, you will find and celebrate your own unique Everyday Soul Dances.

Become quiet and at ease.

Embody the wonderment and the curiosity of a child.

All is possible.

Your true home is in this conscious reuniting with All That Is. Allow this Oneness to permeate your being and to hold your awareness high. I offer both the greatest gifts and the most fearsome challenges. My divinity flows through all experiences equally. Do not doubt your ways, your power, or your passion. You are free to express the gifts of who you are and to enjoy the fruits of these gifts. At this moment, you are beginning a journey in which you will learn to see yourself in your fullness and perfect wholeness. On this path, you will find yourself in forms so infinite and so intimate that your heart will open in joy. You will discover parts of yourself that are so filled with light and so brilliant that your human mind will be dazzled.

I reside in everything. I Am in all colors, in all creative acts, in the arms of love, and all forms of this bountiful universe. I Am in the quiet of the empty mind and in the words you speak.

I Am everywhere.

Absorb Me.

The truth of this moment is stunning. It is brilliant and clear. The next steps you will take along this Soul Dance journey will honor the essence of your spirit. You will be singing songs of your soul that must be sung and dancing inimitable dances that must be danced. This is your magic, and your mystery, and your peerless gift to us all.

This is the story of your soul and your soul's journey. And this is the story of your journey back home to your highest Self.

So Beloved One, thank you for coming to this place, for embarking upon this journey, for longing for Self-discovery, and for being willing to walk the paths that lead to wholeness.

Come.

Pay attention.

Be as gentle as a fawn, as wise as the Goddess, and as courageous as a spiritual warrior. Above all, be your own radiant, free, Divine, and peerless Self.

Remember, above all, that I Am love and these words are the call of your Mother.

Since you are reading this book, you are one of the seekers of sacred living, and you are one of the transformers of the distorted and dark energies of this time. As you enter these ways and dance these graceful dances, know that the great beings shower blessings upon you. I have the utmost respect and gratitude for you, as we know that this time is a chaotic and difficult one. It takes uncommon courage to step beyond the confines of what previously was unknown. This journey is about coming home to yourself, to the gentle and great expressions of your true nature. It is about the discoveries and the recovery of living the life of your soul.

I thank you; for you are one of the ones who will assist in Our world's opening to new and more gentle ways. Doing so is of inestimable value for the world as We know it today.

My Most Beautiful Dear One, welcome home.

Now relax.

Breathe deeply.

Be still and serene.

Listen to My words.

In becoming empty, you hear My silence.
It speaks strongly, softly, gently.
It whispers a call to your name
For I want you

To see Me in everything,
In every experience,
In every way.
And, in this understanding, you find Me
At the very center of your essence.

I call forth your beauty, your magnificence,
Your love, your compassion,
Your strength, and your fluidity
For they are essential
To the balancing
Of the world away from impending destruction.

The time is now.

Know
And honor the greatest,
Which I call you to do.

This is living in its highest form,
Acting from the place of being,
Loving from your golden heart,
Hearing the highest truths in what is spoken,
And sending these truths back out into your world
With your magnificent voice.

Become your passion.
Express your unique colors
Freely, fully,
In sadness,
In joy,
And in delight.

And know, dear people of the mountains,
Of the sands,
Of the waters,
Of the stars, of the moon,

And of the sun
That you are loved, magnified,
Supported, upheld, and enriched
In all you do
For all that you can become
In all times and places.

There is never a way in which I am not.
I am in you and with you.
Flowing through Me, I am expressed through you.

Take time to find Me.

Open.

I am here.

Always.

Forever.

I Am.

You are.

We are One.

HAM SA

CHAPTER 2

INTRODUCTION

In these pages, we will be weaving together strands of ancient yogic ways and current psychological knowledge. In doing so, we will have many opportunities to look at our lives as Everyday Soul Dances. These ways open us to a deeper understanding as to who we are as spiritual beings and as more conscious participants in our daily lives. When we pay close attention to those parts of our lives that work, and those that do not, we learn to embrace that which is of the highest in our daily world. This is our Everyday Soul Dance. Will our moves be conscious and filled with love and lightness of being? Or do we lose our way? And, when we lose our way, what do we do to return to a more conscious and functional state?

You will be invited to explore different aspects of yourself, chapter-by-chapter and step-by-step. The yogic concepts assist us in understanding the broad breadth of what it means to be fully human and spiritual beings simultaneously. Living with such awareness is enlivening and stimulating as our everyday ways become filled with wonder and grace. Your spiritual journey begins here.

The early pages present the words of the Divine Feminine as She invites us to open to Her, to embrace Her, and to embody Her. Then we shift words and context to set the backdrop for what is happening in our world today. Next, the yogic principles of Karma, Dharma, and Destiny remind us of why we are here on this earth at this time. Moving forward, we begin to understand the significance of always living a conscious and spiritual life.

In the next part of the book, we begin to explore specific spiritual and psychological practices that uphold and support us as we move forward in these daily dances. All are about love—of ourselves, of others, our world, the Divine. All these practices are worth noting as you imbibe in their words. You may be more attracted to some than others. So be it. Please listen to the ones that call to you. Create other ways that are unique to you. All these practices are imbued with possibilities for learning, contemplation, and growth.

Along the way, you will have opportunities to listen to, read, and experience meditations relating to various inner practices.

All the parts come together in the third part of the book, as we explore love within the practices that become our daily dances with the Mother within and with others of our communities. Then, finally, we return home to ourselves as manifestations of the Divine.

May you be amazed. May you grow in untold ways and may you enjoy each of these daily steps as you practice them.

CHAPTER 3

THE WAYS OF THIS BOOK

The words of this book honor the Divine Feminine in Her myriad forms. She is our Mother, our teacher, our guide. She lights our ways home to our most sacred Selves. The use of Her voice and Her ways is a conscious one. Her ways are a vivid contrast to the excess of dangerous and negative patriarchal energies that have gone awry in our world today. We experience too much violence, too many wars, too much killing, and too many heartless interactions at the personal level, within our communities, and at the global level. The Divine Feminine energies provide a much-needed counterbalance to these ways. They are necessary for the healing of our world. They are energies for men as well as women. As we grow in consciousness and spiritual receptivity, we embody Her ways and then become Her emissaries—Her hands, Her arms, and Her voices—as we act to change the ways of our world. All of us can learn and grow from Her more gentle and soulful ways.

Her ways, as I know them, have to do with receptivity, openness, and an embrace that encircles every one of us. Her ways are those of gentle nudges, of brilliant insights, of soft and specific teachings. She manifests in abundance, creativity, and soulfulness. She fosters peace—at first within and then without. Her fiery nature and Her firm ways always come from the righting of wrongs, from a need to bring justice and equality to our world, and from a stance that contains the highest truths. We call upon Her when we need to stand up and speak out for ourselves, our families and children, and our brothers and sisters in our communities and worldwide. Each time we do, we are the Goddess in action because She manifests through us.

She wants us to heal, to transform, to love more deeply, and to love many. She holds us in Her grace-filled arms while we live our daily lives. And we all become more open when we learn to relax into Her gentle ways. From there, we form more soulful pathways within ourselves and with one another.

When we align with Her, our vision of what is possible expands, our ways are made clear, and our need to control lessened. Knowing Her, we know others, and we diminish those actions that cause harm to ourselves and others. We become open to making positive changes within our lives. Her embrace and our attention to Her invites greater gentleness as we make such shifts. Each of us is Her emissary, and we each have a vital role to play.

She, our beautiful and radiant Mother, resides within and opens us to Her radiance within our golden hearts. From that centering place, she teaches us more about our essential goodness by sharing Her goodness with us. She wants us to know Her, to live our lives in communion with Her, and to follow Her gentle, loving ways as she teaches us about our inner journeying to find our soulful homes. As we all learn to hold Her close, we bring forth Her divine qualities in our daily lives. Then we become the change bearers, the truth speakers, the soulful leaders so necessary to the righting of our world.

There are different voices in this book. When you read words typed with this font, you are reading my voice. I hope to be a gentle, strong, and evocative guide for you to move more deeply into your most soulful self.

Words printed in this font are the voice of the Divine Feminine, the Mother of Us All, speaking directly to you.

And this font, Dear One, will lead you to your voice. At the end of each chapter, you will be guided into further exploration by suggested questions and contemplations – practices of new ways of living to align with that which is sacred. I hope you will enjoy these contemplations, that you will deepen your experiences of your life as you move ever more into spiritual ways of being.

Be creative and bold. Add your words and ways so that these dances become uniquely yours. Please have a journal dedicated to your Everyday Soul Dances. Your journaling will help with these explorations by offering you ways to refresh your intentions and remember where you came from and who you are. Please know that your own contemplations, words, and experiences will add to these dances to bring you forward into states of expansive strength that will lead you home.

You will find information in this font at the ending of some chapters. It guides you to a related, recorded MEDITATION through QR Code links to the EVERYDAY SOUL DANCES website. Please listen and absorb. The heart of *Everyday Soul Dances* lies in going deep within. These MEDITATIONS will open ways to help you do so. Please have your journal with you as you listen to these words. Contemplating your meditation experiences is a wonderful time to deepen all that is happening within you.

Please revisit your favorite or most needed MEDITATIONS as often as you like.

If you already are on a spiritual path, take a moment to celebrate all that you already know and all that you already practice. You may find that some of the ways in this book are familiar to you and others are new. Take what is useful, expand what you already know, and be curious about new avenues that may be of value to you.

Some of you may be skeptical of the spiritual process. You may think that this book is not for you. Please keep reading if you may have been feeling that you would like to have greater focus in your everyday life, a deeper sense of general contentment, or a need to improve your relationships. Perhaps you have been longing to end the confusion and hyperactivity of your mind or the anxiety and fear that you face. You may find that following some of the words, practices, and meditations in this book will provide you with the answers you are seeking. Please come along.

In our lives, there are always times of despair, times when we experience confusion and anxiety, fear, grief, or guilt—feelings that we often deem as negative, bad, or wrong. On the other hand, there are also times of great joy and deep loving that open us to enthusiasm, expansiveness, and grace. We know these expanded states partially in contrast to the difficult times we experience. We lose our way and then we come back, again and again, contracting and expanding, separating and communing, experiencing waves of anger then waves of understanding, insight, and release.

In between these times of more extreme feelings, there are the many days in which our lives seem ordinary, even dull, or boring. However, if we pay attention to all experiences and emotions, we can ask ourselves, "What can I learn from these?" and "How can I live to enhance my life from one that seems ordinary or troubled into one with joyful intention and grace?" It is in the answers to those questions that we discover how to embrace our spirituality and consciously create lives with less chaos and more spiritual integrity.

The words of this book are gentle reminders that when we walk through the days of our lives, we walk on hallowed ground, we see with sacred eyes, we speak with grace-filled voices, and breathe in the blessings of the gifts that we constantly receive. When we find our ways that deepen life experiences, we reconnect with our essential, sacred Self. We remember that we are a part of All That Is, creating new and sacred pathways with our unique and powerful dances, and our own amazing and brilliant beauty, the beauty of our soul. As we increasingly live our lives from the awareness of our magnificent souls, we know and honor all our acts. Through this newfound self-awareness, we develop a heightened understanding of what others are going through. Then our everyday thoughts and actions become sanctified.

When we step onto the path of *Everyday Soul Dances*, we liberate ourselves from old restrictive habits that no longer serve us while recovering the aspects of ourselves that are our birthright—joy, hope, creativity, and limitless possibilities. From this vantage point, we see how to reconnect with the expansiveness of All That Is. We understand that the larger, eternal, soul-filled Self is who we truly are. At the soul level, we are radiant, pure, and magnificent beyond belief. And every one of us in this lifetime or future ones is moving towards their most brilliant and lighted Selves. When the great beings see us, this lighted Self is who they see.

I hope that this book will be a guide for you to awaken and increasingly open your eyes to this same vision, this same truth: that we can live within a state of immense freedom. When we create within such freedom, all our actions become sacred acts, and we can trust that we are making a grace-filled difference in the world.

We are learning to go further than we have gone before by allowing the sacredness of all spiritual energies to move through us. This means that we will not hold back or be limited in our choices; rather, we will step fully into what it is that we are meant to do. By taking one step at a time, we begin to immerse ourselves in new ways of being that are precious to us.

This book is to be slowly savored, practicing one or two dances until they begin to change your state into one of pure light. All you need to do is to move step by step every day for 90 days or until you have immersed yourself in new ways of living that are precious to you. You can add other dances as you are ready to do so. Always I advocate fluidity, freedom, and fun along with the constancy of your practice. In this way, your spiritual path will be a creative one that is uniquely yours.

PART II

WHAT IS HAPPENING TO US AND OUR WORLD?

CHAPTER 4

THE TIPPING POINT – OLD WAYS AND NEW BEGINNINGS

Despite all the riches and greatness of our society, and all our scientific and technological advances, we still find that parts of the great American dream are found wanting. Many of us have everything we could need in terms of work, relationships, and financial security. Others may lack even the basic necessities for themselves and their families. Some of us are just plain stuck in everyday activities and daily tasks that can seem anything but soul inspired. When any of these conditions are in place, we can easily forget who we truly are. We may feel despair and so very alone hopeless and helpless. While the pressure builds within and without, we try even harder to be in control of our lives and our environments with the resultant eventual breakdown of our physical, emotional, spiritual, and relationship health. This serious breakdown is not unique to any one of us.

Almost daily, we are witnesses to terror and animosity of inconceivable proportions reverberating throughout the world. Many groups of people are left with nothing due to environmental disasters, wars, or misguided leadership. Increasingly we are horrified at the hatred and brutality that sometimes seems to surround us, and we often feel powerless to do anything about any of it. We fear inconceivable experiences, such as complete environmental breakdown and nuclear war. These issues are causing fear, anxiety, and a sense of disbelief in our minds, hearts, and souls like never before. Sometimes we lose our understanding and our way.

Because we do not feel empowered to make changes, we find ourselves individually trapped by our often limited and sometimes extreme concepts of good and evil, a judgmental entrapment that is reflected in the actions of our various societies. When we stay caught in this judgmental thinking, we feel trapped within the limitations of our minds and circumstances. Then these limitations grow exponentially to greater entrapment within our individual lives and our communities.

At one end of the continuum, we are rushing around in hyperactive and frenetic ways; at the other end, we become inert spectators glued to our computers, phones, or TVs. Our focus on technological tools can take priority over loving relationships and deep conversations about who we are to one another. As a result, we lose the ability to love deeply and to communicate fully. We may find that our potentials, along with our fears and pain, stay locked up and hidden within due to a lack of outlets and a lack of support from those who love us. We forsake intimacy and close to our truer Selves and our loved ones.

Because we have so many outer distractions, we may have forgotten what it means to be fulfilled. Our societies, for the most part, do not support our delving deeper into ourselves—into our sacred selves and more intimate connections with others. Therefore, we live in a state of discontent and disconnect, and then we wonder why our lives lack meaning. We have forgotten how to love. We have neglected our communion with our amazing earth, with life's sacredness, and with our divinity. Too often, we have forgotten—or never learned—compassion, humility, deep honoring of ourselves, and abiding respect of and empathy for others.

If we believe that our diminished state is all there is, we become stagnant and resigned to living in smaller ways and with a sense of hopelessness. We fear that we no longer are enough. We may give our power away to others and then discover that those others cannot lead us on to higher and better ways of being. The truth is that we have forgotten our values and histories that are rich in the spiritual underpinnings that contain the knowledge of how to return to a more enlightened state. Yet despite our amnesia, we sense that there must be something more, something better in our lives to fulfill our purpose in being here.

Sometimes it takes surviving difficult life circumstances to find that purpose. It is often in those times of strife and crises that we do our most courageous growing. Throughout all our lives, we suffer and strive, then accept and learn as we learn how to thrive.

A friend tells me that we are at a tipping point. She strongly states that each of us must do our part because we are all interconnected. Everyone and everything affects every other one and every other thing as energies shift with our actions. She says that if we sell ourselves short, we sell the world short and let ourselves and others down. We are being called to become more and more conscious, more courageous, and more and more careful in how we treat each other, our beautiful planet, and ourselves. We also are being called to stand up for truth and righteousness, and to live and act from spiritual qualities in all that we do to counterbalance the ways of anger, hatred, violence, and destruction that seem so prevalent now.

So, the vital question is: *"How do we make such shifts to begin to right the wrongs within ourselves and our communities?"* One answer is that we must discover how to turn our ordinary acts into sacred acts by shifts in perspective and action. As a start, we can embrace a higher sense of who we are by attending to our daily tasks from a place of deep humility, honor, and an ever-deepening connection with the beauty and magnificence of All That Is. As we grow in these ways and connect at deeper levels with our spiritual essence, our more negative states lessen, and we find ourselves free of hopelessness, anger, and other psychological difficulties. And, as we live in more open and loving ways, we become sacred emissaries with newfound energies that flow out into the world. Each of us becomes a gift, and our very being shines out to light the way for others to become their better, more loving, and inspired selves.

Some of us may be learning to love for the very first time. As this new relationship with love grows, it becomes easier and less daunting to find solutions to societal ills, first within ourselves, then within our families and communities, and then within the larger structure of our global community. Our new experience with real love is helping us eliminate the lesser beliefs of separation and duality, and the burden and boundaries of black and white thinking. As we open to our spiritual essences, we discover what we are here to do. We are here to take responsibility for what we create. We are here to speak out when others are being harmed. We are here to find our spiritual foundations, and then live our lives with these new viewpoints in place as much as possible every day. In so doing we experience transparency and cooperation. All these new attributes give us the power to make a strong commitment to finding solutions that are far more generous and sustaining than much of what we have in place today.

We are here to be light bearers in a world with too much darkness.

Once we understand the sacred interconnections of a truly global community, we will learn to embrace love rather than hate and to embrace peace rather than settling for anger or isolation. As clear and true as this corollary is, there often are personal challenges that we must address before we can embody love and peace. In one case we must let go of an old experience; in the other, we will embrace a new one.

The first challenge we face is the release of old, ego-bound beliefs that create duality, lesser consciousness, and limitations. These habitual thoughts have been a part of us for lifetimes, and they are what contribute to our difficult karmic experiences in the present. When we act out of greed, envy, addiction, anger, covetousness, judgment, and other habitual negative patterns, we are still in ego-based states of right and wrong, good and bad, and a sense of self-righteousness that keeps us stuck. Addressing these lesser patterns is the work of psychotherapy and transformative spiritual practices.

The second challenge is to learn to embrace Divine Consciousness, the Mother, the Holy Spirit, and our own higher consciousness. We do this by living soulful lives that are vital, embracing, and deeply connecting. In releasing old limiting approaches to our lives and by embodying new expansive beliefs in their place, we learn to become more loving, and awe inspired with All That Is. In these ways, we contribute to much-needed change within our world.

When we walk through the days of our lives, we walk on sacred ground; we see with sacred eyes, speak with hallowed voices, and breathe in the blessings of Divine Consciousness. Once we know this to be true, we can embrace our essential, sacred Selves, and understand that as we live, we create, with and without words, our new and brilliant ways, our unique and powerful dances, and our own amazing and luminous beauty. As we increasingly live our lives from the awareness of our magnificent souls, we know and honor all our acts. Then they become sacred, and our ways contain a quiet beauty that is sacredness itself.

We are energetic beings connected to the Divine and a pantheon of angels, saints, other ascended masters, and healers. There is much more to us than we can imagine. Therefore, we are much greater than our embodied physical selves and our often cut-off defeated emotional selves. Once we experience the expanded Self, we know ourselves to be beautiful beings brimming full of potential. Then we begin to have a different sense of the possibilities of who we are and of who others are as well.

As your mind and body expand into this consciousness of All That Is, you will learn to stay centered no matter the external circumstances—even during situations that can be stressful, chaotic, fragmented, and exceedingly difficult. Our soulful rhythms will become our truer nature. We will rest more at ease within ourselves, and our hearts and minds will more easefully connect with one another. Then we will find, amazingly, that anything we choose to do becomes a part of the rich, beautiful, and sacred tapestry that is the dance of our life.

The more we embody our soul-filled natures, the more we realize our interconnection with each other and with this amazing universe. The more we can love, the less we fall prey to our ego's designs, dis-eases, addictions, and emotional malaise. So, together, let us gracefully dance into new and inspired ways of being. In doing so, we will live new, better, and more extraordinary lives. We do this day by day and in any and every situation. It is in daily observation and contemplation that we learn more about ourselves and can begin to access the spiritual dimensions through actions that embody spiritual qualities. These are the positive qualities of compassion, love, fearlessness, faith, trust, commitment, and constancy.

Any person, experience, or message from the natural world can be our teacher. We learn to open our eyes wider, to keep the focus soft, and then to ask, "What is it that I am meant to experience and to learn at this moment?" One of the things we will be learning through this yogic perspective is that we cannot predict the outcome of our actions. Instead, it is the action itself and the way it is performed that contains the value. As you begin to live your life with increasing awareness, attention, and love, you will be amazed at how the universe rises to meet you in ways that you previously could not have imagined.

So, go for it! Each time and each way are perfect for your learning and your soul development. *All* your experiences, the ordinary, everyday ones, the sacred and magnificent ones, even the difficult ones—the ones that bring you to your knees—are full of potential once you learn to pay attention to the messages contained within. Congratulate yourself for your successes and commit to correcting your course when necessary, especially when the issue involves an unanticipated and perhaps unpleasant interaction with one of your teachers. When that happens, be extremely gentle with yourself, non-judgmental, forgiving, and accepting of exactly who you are and who the other person is at any moment. We never know the karmic underpinnings that we are destined to live in this life. Send love to every person, including yourself, and especially to those who seem problematic for you. Remember, that, despite and because of the difficulties, these people are your teachers. They too are finding their own ways. Commit to understanding each lesson and learning it well. In this way, you create karma that is more wonderful for yourself and your future in this life and the next ones. As you learn and grow, you will find that you are living a sacred life, moment by moment and that it is good.

What happens when the moment for a course correction comes? If you are following the path of *Everyday Soul Dances*, you have learned some steps that can guide you to a better course. Sometimes, though, new directions do not appear right away; they may seem elusive. Often in those moments, you may experience some challenging human emotions. Please know that it is normal to be afraid, sometimes to the point of questioning how you can go on. Of course, you will question, want to run away, pull back, or perhaps revert to old patterns for a short or even longer time. We all can run from the places that frighten us. In the moment, these diversions may be tempting and comforting. They provide immediate escape and feel so good—until they no longer do. Then there is the next day and the next, and another story—emptiness, dullness, self-recrimination, a sense of failure, and fatigue.

Eventually, and yet again, the longing for a better way will find you. These energies live within you—beyond your fear. You can count on it. However, learn to trust that your fears become motivators for change and that when you find the path you are to follow, your fear will evaporate. Eventually, and again, you will come face to face with your higher Self, the part of you that whispers or even shouts that there is so much more to you and your life. The longing for that course correction urges you to listen. It never gives up.

These messages may come in many forms, some that startle you into awakening.

> *Oh. Here it is again- the Mystery - the Mother - God -*
> *Goddess - Life in its fullness.*

You stop and breathe deeply in awe. You listen, and you take note of that message.

> *Oh! I am conscious! I am connected! I am home and it is*
> *good. This is where I truly belong.*

These messages contain a truth that you need to hear. You know that each one is a sacred message, the perfect one for you at this moment. Often the message contains the challenge you are meant to meet. By paying attention, you remember who you truly are and the knowledge that there is more that life is asking of you now. This knowing becomes a longing to meet the challenge. Then you understand that you must follow this longing, even without knowing exactly what it is, where it will lead, or what will be asked of you along the way.

> You say... *"I must do this despite my fear. I am being led*
> *by the Great Mystery as it resounds in my life. This is a*
> *sacred moment. Nothing else is as important. My answer*
> *is "YES."*

In doing so, you re-claim your strength, your faith and courage, and your capacity for acting, remembering that you always have these attributes. The truth of this moment is stunning. It is brilliant and clear. At this moment, you know that you have come home to your Self, and to that which is divine. And, you know that with this next step you take, you will honor the truth of your spirit. You will be singing the songs of your soul that must be sung. This is the magic, and the mystery, of the spiritual journey.

This is a journey that requires attention and courage, and a commitment to Self that is well worth the effort. Our beings are hungry for a return to wholeness. This is a time to be strong and even fiery when necessary, to be humble always, and to radiate compassion toward all our brothers and sisters. This is a time to speak out against untruths and injustices, to care for those who are feeling broken, and to touch others in our most loving ways.

As we move forward within these new ways, our days become lighter, more loving, and serene. In living from our highest potential, we are each a part of the healing solutions for our families, our communities, and our world. When we make these changes our world benefits, as these new energies flow from us to those in our lives who are ready to receive them.

So, Dear One, do not doubt the power of your impact on a seemingly broken world. Thank you for coming to this place, for embarking upon this journey, for longing for deeper self-discovery, and for being willing to take the steps that lead you into wholeness. This journey is about coming home to yourself, to the gentle, creative, strong, and loving expressions of your true nature as you move through this most beautiful life. It is about finding a deep peace within no matter what is happening around you, and above all, it is about living in loving ways in all of life's circumstances.

Absorb these words, act on the ones that most call to you, and enjoy the wonders along the way!

CONTEMPLATION

Now it is your turn.

Take your journal and reflect upon what you have just read. Was there something in the words that particularly touched you? If so, write about it.

How do you already successfully cope and recover from stressors?

If you experience stressful patterns that concern you, what needs to be shifted and what support do you need?

In the next few days, continue to contemplate these questions and your answers.

Write as much and as often as you like.

PART III

WELCOME TO THE LAND OF YOUR KARMA, YOUR DHARMA, AND YOUR DESTINY

CHAPTER 5

YOUR SOULS JOURNEY

My Beloved,

Your story is ancient, magnificent, as deep as the oceans, and as large as the cosmos. Think about this. Is it not a wonder that so much is contained within? The soul's longing for the Divine resides within you. You may not be familiar with it yet. You may have inklings of new ways and new possibilities, or you may be ready to burst forth. Any such messages are calls from Me penetrating your consciousness to remind you of our communion. These calls ask you to step beyond ordinary ways of being. They are calls to remember that you are an eternal, radiant light being. Once you awaken to these truths, you will find that you are My emissary, My hands, My voice, and My ways. I enter your world through you. When this happens, the ordinary ways of existence diminish as you are increasingly open to all that you are and to the sanctity that swirls within you and beyond you.

This communion in each moment is stunning for it always means that We come together in love. Together We dissolve worn ways and decrease negative karma so that your light may become brighter and all-pervasive; then you heal yourself and the world around you.

One of the ways to begin to make sense of your unique part in this amazing universe is to embrace the consciousness of All That Is. This embrace is strong yet delicate and subtle. It is an embrace of the heart, of your entire being, and your soul-filled nature. This embrace is the far-reaching dance of your life. It is to be nurtured and expanded so that you might open your heart to the good and magnificent within and find the means to embrace that which is difficult. The energy underlying all that we are and all that we experience is the universal life force or Divine Consciousness. This energy permeates all things, all people, and all parts of the universe. Within this energy, every one of us is connected to all others and to the brilliance of the cosmos. While this energy is difficult to know through our highly active minds, we tap into it when we quiet our mind and open it to spiritual dimensions. Then we know the wonderment of this energy as our true home, the place from which we came and to which we return again and again.

According to ancient yogic texts,[1] we each have access to the archetypal consciousness that forms themes and patterns that are available to us yet surpasses our everyday human understanding. Therefore, this universal consciousness tamps itself down to become small enough for an individual's consciousness to grasp, which, paradoxically, is also limitless. We also contain within our energetic bodies all of the accumulated karma from previous lifetimes and specific karmas that are meant to be experienced during this current life. When we incarnate as individual souls within unique bodies, we come with specific sets of circumstances and a unique personality and physicality that will serve as the vehicle for our soul's journey in this lifetime. With the practice of the various forms of yoga, we can learn to work with these energies within ourselves, and, in the process, create profound healing at many levels of our being.

You will find that as you grow in this awareness and become free of the denser constrictions of the personality, the ego, and the karmic conditions of this lifetime, you will feel lighter. With this new awareness, you can reclaim the lighted truth of your being at higher energy frequencies, in which you live more and more from your soul, from your true center. In this new state of being, you become increasingly aware of the guidance and connections coming from the non-physical realms. This divine help is your natural birthright, and it aids you in living from your highest potential. And as part of All That Is, you become part of the upliftment of all of humanity. All of us who are yearning and searching for more enlightened ways of being bring incredible, vital, and much-needed healing to our planet. It is for this that we have been born.

But, what of the negative karmic patterns that are also present in this transformative time? We usually need to do inner work to counterbalance the negative karmic conditioning within ourselves and the difficult patterns of others whose consciousness may be bound by patterns of good and evil, right and wrong. Once we step into a space of interconnectedness with all of life, we become very humble. When we come from this place, we are living our lives at the highest possible frequencies of love and truth; we know that we are acting from our limitless potential and that we are doing genuinely good work for our world. Living from such expanded vision in communion with the Divine sets the stage for us to change our destiny to one that is limitless and in perfect alignment with the rest of the world. Then it is also possible to be in relationships with the Divine Mother, the angels, saints, and other ascended masters. Once we know and live with this sense of oneness, we are free.

According to the ancient Sanskrit texts, and illuminated by Gary Zukav,[2] your soul and all souls are eternal aspects of the Divine Consciousness. All souls, throughout lifetimes, eventually partake of this journey and return home to their original and lighted Selves. This growth is a natural progression necessary for our evolution and the evolution of all humankind. When we understand the vagaries of each person's journey during any given lifetime, we can let go of our expectations and judgments. Rather than expecting others to meet our standards, instead, we simply learn to focus our attention on taking fully conscious responsibility for our own choices. Then we learn to contemplate how these ways either serve us or need correcting. As we evolve ever more consciously, we cannot help but influence those around us. In this way, all evolve.

This is the soul's dance:

- To become conscious of ourselves as soul-infused people living a spiritual life in a more ordinary world.

- To understand and heal patterns of living and patterns of the personality that do not serve the journey of the soul.

- To replace these less conscious patterns with ones that hold spiritual qualities of love and light.

- To live from this place of ever-growing freedom and capability.

33

As you increasingly enter such soul-filled ways of being, you will make unique contributions to your world.

Some of the healers and psychics who see the broad breadth of soul development speak of the soul's communication with its guides between lifetimes. According to these seers, during this in-between time, the individual soul and its guides assess what was learned in previous lifetimes and what needs to be experienced for the soul's growth in the current one. Then particular sets of circumstances are established and agreed upon that will contribute to new growth. Based upon this information, in between one incarnation and the next one, we choose parents and families who will best provide the specific sets of experiences we need for our soul's growth in each lifetime. Our chosen family members agree, at the soul level, to serve in this way, even if their roles are beyond our conscious understanding or theirs. Once we know more about our karma and that of those around us, it is easier to be aware of the importance of how we live our lives and to amend any negative judgments about how others are living theirs.

When we incarnate, the dramas begin. Our souls know the paths we are to walk and the dreams and life we are to create. We can see these ways in the souls of little ones early on. As a child grows in physicality and into the realities of this world, the soul memories fade, and the child's earth-based personality begins to develop, providing a forum of experiences for growth and learning. When we understand this journey from the perspective of the soul, each experience, each person, and each turn of anger, jealousy, fear, depression, and love are aspects of the lessons we need to learn and experience. However, one cannot fully understand these lessons without bringing a conscious appreciation of the soul into the picture. Between souls, there is only love. Person to person, there usually is much to evolve.

On the earth plane, we can experience ways within ourselves and within our relationships that are non-loving and often seemingly beyond our capacity to understand or change. However, once we become familiar with the beauty and purposefulness of our increasing awareness through soul work, divine understanding becomes part of our human experience. Then, with some new knowledge of who we all are, these daily interactions become infused with soul-filled qualities that take on greater importance and new meanings. In this way, we clear karma and become wiser in our ways. We are forever changed. These changes will always affect our relationships although not always in ways that we could have predicted. This is because the soul's path teaches through loving and not loving until our loving deepens and we spiral home to our sacred Selves. When we take responsibility for ourselves rather than falling into victim states, we are acting on what we know to be true from the sacred space of our hearts. We can address any negative karma by apologizing, making amends, forgiving ourselves and others, and living in new and more enlightened ways. If our human experiences have led us to difficult psychological conditions and/or addictions, we can get the necessary treatment to release life circumstances that have kept us stuck in self-destructive patterns. As all this transpires, our communications become much clearer, and we begin to welcome opportunities to communicate deeply with others. We then find joy in using our talents and intelligence, creating our lives consciously, and living spiritual truths as we develop them within ourselves.

Elaine Hoem

CONTEMPLATION

Write about your first experience of knowing that there was something beyond yourself that amazed you or settled you into a deeper appreciation of yourself, your spirituality, and your world.

.

Write about your spiritual journey since then.

CHAPTER 6

KARMA

In a word, karma equals action. According to many ancient spiritual traditions, in any given lifetime, our thoughts and our actions generate energetic forces that shape our destiny. Each one of us carries karmic seeds of past impressions that are stored within our energetic bodies until the right karmic conditions come together. Then openings occur in our lives for this karma to be played out. A simple analogy is that we each hold a deck of karmic cards at the beginning of a lifetime. These cards carry within them the possibilities for our dharma and our destiny. The questions contained within them are *"Will we fold because our karmic circumstances seem too hard?"* or *"Will we take this karmic deck and do what needs to be done to have the most positive and successful life possible?"* When we choose the latter way, we release old karmic patterns and consciously establish new ways of living that are more consciously aware. Thus, healing occurs, often at all levels of our being.

THE LAW OF KARMA

We learn in basic physics that "For every action, there is an equal and opposite reaction." The Law of Karma echoes this truth. It is the law of cause and effect. Whenever we act, our action will generate another action in response. No person is ever exempt from this law. Although we often hear about Karma from the perspective of the negative, as in "He must have bad Karma," it is just as often a response of positivity. For instance, as we become conscious, more aware, and more loving, our lives, which were once lacking in all those attributes to one degree or another, become more radiant, graceful, and connected to the Divine and others. We live with more ease and become clearer in our choices. As we recognize what is happening, we can applaud our self-efforts and the changes we see in others to acknowledge our appreciation for the abundant gifts that we receive when we lead a spiritual life. This too is the result of the Law of Karma.

At its best, The Law of Karma guarantees the right action in the present moment. This tenet of the Law, therefore, explains how our talents and life circumstances lead us to certain work, certain places to live, and certain people who will be our teachers along the way. When we learn to respect this Law and pay conscious attention to each opportunity that comes our way, we are aware that no matter what our first inclinations might be, some experiences and some people are right for us. These circumstances and relationships need exploration. With other people and in other situations, the opposite might be true. As we increase our discernment of this Law through a closer connection with the Divine, we move with more certainty in the directions that are drawing us to people and situations that will uplift us or teach us. By doing so, these connections guide us further into the true nature of our spiritual selves and therefore closer to our inner relationship with the Divine. This is the beautiful unfolding of the Law of Karma.

The principles of Karmic law continue throughout all our lives.[3] This means that we will eventually experience the karmic consequences of our actions, either in the life in which they were created or in future ones. Sometimes, we can see an immediate karmic effect, especially when it is a more challenging one; other times, the effect is more subtle, but we can rest assured that the results of our actions will occur at some point in our lifetimes. This is true for karma experienced as either negative or positive. And just as negative karma can build upon previous negative karma so does positive karma build upon itself.

Many ancient texts describe the types of karma. In most if not all these texts, with some variation, Vedic writers (c. 500–1500 BCE) described three types of karma. They may vary in complexity and the use of differing Sanskrit terms.[4]

Prarabdha Karma is karma that is responsible for certain conditions that we carry within a particular life. These karmas usually cannot be avoided or changed. These energies create certain conditions that we will live out—where we live, our family, conditions of the world around us, and physical and personality conditions that we are born with. For the most part, such conditions are not subject to change.

Sanchita Karma is karma from past lives that we bring into this one. With this type of karma, we have choices. When we take the high road with the circumstances we are presented with, we are creating positive karma and may be eliminating the karmic debt that we have been carrying. This karma has far-reaching effects as we may be clearing karma that has been a part of our ancestral makeup for generations. Thus, by living in conscious ways, we are helping to resolve karma for our ancestors and so that our children will no longer carry such burdens.

Kriyaman Karma is the karma we create in the present. This karma can be both positive and negative. It will create future karma. We have control over the creation of this type of karma. Spiritual practices such as meditation, prayer, service to others, and union with our Higher Self affect our *Kriyaman Karma*, dissolving other lesser karmas so that they do not bear fruit in the future.

When we do not deal with destructive patterns that we carry in this life, we can guarantee that we will experience similar patterns at a future point in time until we learn the psychological and spiritual lessons necessary for our soul's growth.

An example to further explain all this is as follows: A child may be born with a severe disability. This is her *Prarabdha Karma.* How she and those around her address her disability becomes their *Sanchita Karma.* And this is where the challenges lie for the child, her family, and her community. If all successfully meet the challenges and act from high and loving ways, they, most likely, will not be creating similar karma to be resolved in future lives. If, however, one of the caretakers abuses this child, this person will have other karmic challenges of a similar nature in future times until she learns more conscious and loving ways. Either way, these caretakers will be setting the stage for their *Kriyaman Karma* in the future.

For our soul's growth, it is right that we pay attention to our karmic conditions. If we do not undertake this work in this lifetime, we will have similar challenges and opportunities in future ones. Our soul's journey involves finding and living within our beautiful sacred Self. This means that we do the necessary soul work to stand clear and strong in our sense of worthiness so that Divine Consciousness can freely express through us.

Again, all that we are and all that we create become a part of our soul's journey through lifetimes. Therefore, if we long to be free, we will grow, psychologically and spiritually. When we do such deep and thoughtful work, we are relieving ourselves of difficult karmic conditions. When our life ends, many of the past karmas that were a part of us in this life also end.

When we realize that we are spiritual beings living in human bodies, we become aware that we need to strive to be conscious of all our choices to stay focused on this beautiful soul journey. As this happens, we are undoing previous negative karma, healing issues that may have plagued us for lifetimes, and stepping forward into our most beautiful and Divinely connected selves.

We are magnificently complex, multidimensional beings. Within each of us are lofty spiritual qualities, some hidden and some not. We also contain the potentiality for creativity, love, and expressive connections greater than the ways we are currently living. Yet we also all have shadow selves, those parts of ourselves we do not want to acknowledge. We want them to stay hidden from ourselves and others. When shadow sides come to the fore, life often becomes difficult for us and for those with whom we share relationships. However, when we pay attention to these parts of ourselves that are not a part of how we like to see ourselves, we create opportunities for learning.

If we do not understand and do not face up to the challenges our shadow self presents to us, we may continue in the same destructive patterns that will lead to more negative karmic conditions. In other words, when we stay in our small, ego-bound selves and do not reflect upon all that we are, we may be doing our world and ourselves a disservice. If we do not grow now, when will we? When negative karmic conditions are rectified and released, that pattern of karma is resolved. It is over and does not result in accumulations of further such karma in this life or the next ones. This, then, is one of the gifts of increased awareness and soul work. Its effects are felt within and have a great impact on our world at large.

Knowing all of this, it can be difficult for us to understand why, in the land of our karma for all lifetimes, some of us seem to experience little spiritual growth for reasons that only one's soul knows. We may question why there are people who continue in their destructive ways and people who seem unable to take responsibility for their actions. However, once we realize that there are specific karmic reasons for each of us living in the ways that we do, it is easier to be at ease with others who are making choices that we do not understand. There are many instances when even knowing what we know about karma, it is easier to understand what it might take to make such a change. The extremely challenging experiences of depression, anxiety, PTSD, addictions, illnesses, and low self-esteem are difficult ones to heal. They create debilitating pain and suffering that makes any action extremely hard to take. They keep us bound in that pain unless we find the inner strength to use these very human conditions as springboards into conscious wellness and consciousness-raising that will create in us a longing for more whole and wholesome ways of being. The ability to move from a lesser state to a greater one is where our work and our beauty lie. This continuous dance can be denied but ultimately not circumvented if we are to become more joyfully and fully ourselves. This is the yogic dance of karma as we dance living small and then leaping into greatness.

Part of the spiritual journey is that in any given lifetime, we have amazing highs and difficult lows. Often it is these lows— our illnesses, our relationship problems, our losses, addictions, and adversities—that open gateways for old karma to come forth and for greater healing to take place. Karma plays itself out in our destiny and our relationships. When we embrace a conscious spiritual path, we begin to use these experiences for contemplation to expand our sense of our selves. During the difficult times, and often, during the amazing times, we may be open to receiving help from others—the wise ones, the transpersonal therapists, and the healers—who can help us understand the much larger and sacred patterns that are running through our lives. When we look at these patterns, at the

41

parts of ourselves that do not fit with our positive perceptions of ourselves, the work of clearing our karma comes forth to be healed.

With the right kinds of spiritual and psychological help, we can learn to integrate these problematic parts, for example, to accept that we too have shadow selves and that we will take responsibility to brings these parts into awareness to be able to understand and integrate them with the rest of our personality. Then we easily bow in humility when faced with others' shadow sides, as we know that we all are fallible and that the arms of the Divine Mother embrace us all.

When we hold onto these problems without self-examination, problematic living may overtake us. Then we may have years of bitterness, disaffection, dis-ease, malaise, and a lack of ability to cope well. We may have a sense of false pride and self-righteousness despite the disruptions such behaviors cause in our lives and the lives of those around us until, through one way or another, we become conscious, do deep inner work, forgive ourselves, forgive others, and come to understand how these choices were a part of the growth of this lifetime. When we are on the other side of these changes, the past choices and the resultant negative dynamics dissipate from all levels of our being. At times, it is necessary to revisit these karmic patterns, again and again, spiraling around to deeper and deeper levels while each time reaching and releasing another layer of karma.

Our karmas and our destinies connect us all. Any suffering or trauma felt by a person or group of people affects all of us. We experience these connections most evenings when we watch the news and grieve over the travesties and horrors that occur throughout the world. We are not separate from the suffering, pain, and violence of any other person or group of people.

In this lifetime or in past ones, we too have been the priestesses, the "witches," the benevolent leaders and the corrupt ones, the serfs, the masters, and the slaves. Our lifetimes are many. Within them, we played both noble roles and those roles that have hurt others and ourselves. We may have more than once acted out negative patterns we see in others today—the disparaging of others and the devaluing of others. At times, in our healing journeys, we may be able to see into these lifetimes and these actions to clear the negative energies and then to heal and to release them. When this happens, we can no longer say, "I would never do something like that" because we hold the memories of what we have done. The healing work is to see the truth of who we were, to see how others may have been involved, to honor and express the related feelings, to release the energies living within, and then to forgive ourselves and the others who were involved. The release of these energies usually happens in hypnotherapy, in the hands of a skilled and far-seeing healer, or through transformative spiritual experiences. Once the distorted energies are gone, they are gone. Then that piece of karma is over.

In each of us, there is a longing for the light, for a return home to our multidimensional God/Goddess-infused selves. Eventually, we all will find our ways home, in one lifetime or another. During this lifetime, we have so much support available. Why not now? Why not choose to grow further, to become more conscious, to heal, to embrace our greatness, and to undo past negative karmas we have created? In doing so, we flow into our goodness, our joy, our beauty, our love, and our unlimited potential. We each have a contribution to make in this cosmic tapestry we call life. Our unique and precious strand interweaves with those of all others for our learning in inimitable ways. When we undertake this task, we serve those around us and add our radiance and clarity to the much-needed light in our world.

In these times, with the growth of expanded consciousness in all parts of the world, we have the gift of knowing the great beings among us, alive or ascended, who can assist us in cutting the knots of karma—the gurus, saints, angels, and healers. We need to do our individual psychological work, and we can also ask for assistance from all those guides as well as from the Mother, the Holy Spirit, and the ascended masters with whom we are connected. Any clearing that we do brings us closer to our divinity and draws us forward toward our sacred destiny.

Always there will be much more to the story. The good news is that any joy and expression of beauty also reflects throughout. We know that we are not alone, and we have untold opportunities to connect with other like-minded people who are also searching for their true home within. Our soulful prayers are heard, and our voices and our healings expand outward to touch many others. Everything we do has consequences for ourselves and others.

Therefore, it makes good sense to grow, to undo negative karma, and to give our best for the sake of our destiny and the sake of our world. It is then that we can bow in deep humility with gratitude and the wonder of it all.

Why not say "Yes!" to it all now?

> *Several years ago, I had the experience of participating in a Family Constellation workshop. In this group experience, one person tells of a problem s/he is having. The leader selects different group participants to take the roles of those involved in the family drama, including one person stepping in for the person with the problem. It is mostly silent work except for prompts and questions by the leader. Each role-player takes on the body language of the feelings s/he is having as is befitting to their roles. The feelings are often dramatic, and the body postures are as well.*
>
> *In this constellation, a man was having horrible wartime nightmares, even though neither he nor his father had ever been in a war. However, the father's father had fought in World War II and returned from this war with "shell shock", but it was something that he never talked about to either his son or his grandson.*
>
> *The leader chose people to play the man in the constellation, his wife, his father, and his grandfather. As soon as these people assumed their roles and the resulting body positions that illustrated their feelings, a pall descended over the room. We all felt a sense of despair—brokenness, and hopelessness.*
>
> *In the constellation, the father was closed off and looking away. The spouse felt helpless yet was reaching out and wanting to help. The person playing the role of the man with the nightmares was hunched over and afraid. The grandfather fell to the floor, wounded and overtaken by both his physical wound and long-lasting psychological symptoms known today as post-traumatic stress syndrome (PTSD). The grandson turned and watched, eyes wide open, seeing the truths of his granddad's experience. The grandson sobbed at the horrors of it all, at the silence of the generations, and at his finally understanding what his dreams were all about. In this transformative moment, the familial karma dissipated. His wife no longer had to be hyper-vigilant and was able to step back from worry. Later we found out that this man's nightmares had ceased. Doing this work served not only him but also the other members of his family and lineage.*

CONTEMPLATION

Now you get to illustrate these words with ideas from your life.

What are some obvious karmic circumstances that run through this lifetime?
Past?

Present?

Future?

Give examples of times when your actions were of the highest and you knew that you were creating good karma.

What are your next steps in releasing negative karma and enacting positive karma?

CHAPTER 7

EMBRACING YOUR DHARMA

Dharma is a concept handed down over time with initial references found in the *Bhagavad Gita* when Lord Krishna was instructing the warrior Arjuna about the necessity of doing his duty despite his fear and despair.[5] These sections of this text provide us with both ancient and modern teachings about living in strong and courageous ways despite our fears and circumstances. Spiritual texts in many traditions contain similar truths. The outer manifestations of dharma consist of noble principles of living such as justice, honesty, peaceful ways, respect for self and others, and service to others.

At the personal level, I like to think of dharma as the creation of our lives in high and conscious ways as we walk those paths that bring us into greater harmony and fullness. For some, this path is clear early on. For others, we find our ways through one experience after another. A spiritual longing helps to define our roles in any given lifetime. When we act in dharmic ways, we change our destinies to better, more enlightened ones. A dharmic life begins with an intention followed by appropriate action. It always has to do with concern for the highest good for others involved as well as for our good.

I find that there are at least three aspects to such a life. The first is doing the best we can do in any situation and speaking in compassionate and loving ways in every moment. Each time we pay attention and act from the highest good, we create positive karma that has increasingly larger effects throughout this lifetime and into future ones. Our holding a high state of awareness also reverberates throughout our world and touches others in ways we may not consciously know. Eventually these acts and the grace that follows lead us to the numinous, to the presence of divinity, and our more sacred Selves as we live in communion with the ways of the Divine. As we continue to live our lives with a sense of wonder and refinement, and as we learn to work through difficult problems with greater understanding and ease, we become clearer about who we truly are. This freedom, then, is a gift of Spirit that we have created for ourselves.

The second explanation of dharma honors our unique contribution—the gifts, talents, and abilities we share with our world. Sometimes, these gifts are evident early in a person's life. Other times, we become familiar with them as we grow, have different experiences, and then learn from such experiences. When we recognize that our offerings are our contribution to the world, we want to augment our endeavors to live a dharmic life. We do not let obstacles diminish us. We move forward on this path because it is so very right for us. We may find that doorways open in brilliant and unexpected ways. Then our work becomes our dharma, our lives our offerings, and our ways filled with grace.

The third aspect of dharma that seems vital to understand because of our very full lives is that of doing the best we know how to do and maintaining a harmonious balance in all that we do. As I see it, dharma relates to our life's work. It has to do with how we love—how we are with our communities, our Earth, and all Her creatures. All that we do in our daily lives becomes a part of our dharma when we act with consciousness. When we pay close attention, we practice how to balance the days of our lives among the areas of family, work, self-reflection, and play. Dharma also involves spiritual study and spiritual practices. If we are to dance our way to our most sacred Selves, we will find both challenges and accomplishments through these amazingly complementary acts.

However, gaining this balance is not always easy to figure out or to put into action. We may need to alter our paths in both small and large ways. Sometimes we must work through difficult situations with others. And, if difficult relationships warrant that we must stay, we are called upon to explore how to make such circumstances the backdrop for our learning to become more conscious. Then we correct course to make changes for the good of all involved. At other times, we need to ask for help from another to find an outcome that is greater than our current thinking allows. And there are also times when the answer is that it may be best to turn away and leave a particular situation when circumstances worsen, and we have lost our way.

Making these sometimes-difficult changes requires great courage, the willingness to do things differently in any area of our lives, and the longing to live in more creative, expansive ways. The further we delve into these yogic balances, the less separation we will find and the deeper our communion with all beings. Along the way, we replace anxiety and fear with compassion and a sense of rightness in the way we live our lives. In the spiritual realms, there are no wars, no ethnic cleansings, and no rejections of the other; rather, there is only connection, humility, and gratitude. We know at the deepest level that all people feel what happens to any one of us.

One simple contemplation that I have found helpful is to ask ourselves the following questions in any large or small situation in which we have mixed feelings.

What is the highest way for me to act or speak in this situation?

How will my choice benefit others as well as myself?

What way will move me forward on my spiritual path?

What choices will be for the greatest good of all involved?

Often it is important to journal about these dilemmas, to talk with a wise friend, to pray, and to meditate to find clarity. Once you have reflected on your questions in these ways, sit in meditation. Imagine dropping your mind with its question down into your heart. Hold it close and be open to receiving a heart-infused answer. When your answer comes from both mind and heart, there will be a resounding sense of rightness. Then your direction will be clear. The answers may or may not come immediately; however, as you continue to hold your questions within the space of your mind and heart, the answers will come.

When we are living in dharmic ways, we are living lives filled with integrity and goodness. We are creating positive karmic conditions that dissolve negative karmic seeds lying dormant within us from past times. When we do what we love and what brings us joy, we are living dharmic lives. When we grow into a vision of what we must do, we are growing into our dharma. Once we are clear about our dharmic paths, it is good to keep moving forward and always aim to get back on the path if we lose our way. Sometimes this requires great focus to act from our highest dharmic possibilities more consistently. However, the rewards are worthy of our efforts. As we learn to move beyond our fearful places, pay loving attention to all that we do, and correct course along the way, we can embrace and enjoy an ever-increasing commitment to our spiritual journeys, and an ever-deepening love and acceptance for ourselves and others.

Growing into our dharma is our spiritual journey. It may take a lifetime or lifetimes. Always, as we do this, we are in communion with the dances and songs of our soul. We become more connected with the light of higher consciousness as we act from love in service to our world. Each act then becomes a sacred act that changes our destiny and uplifts those around us and beyond. It is as simple as that. The gifts along the way are profound, often unexpected, and always have to do with opening more to the Divine, with freedom, soulfulness, and joy.

Here is a story from my life that illustrates how choices we make early on may have profound effects upon the weaving of our lives.

Early in my career, after graduate work in psychology, I was working at a center for disabled children and their families. The work was satisfying, an outgrowth of my previous work in institutions for disabled people. We offered programs that helped people in the community in many ways. The staff was vibrant and creative. I was learning, growing, and content.

Then an unexpected door opened with an offer for me to shift to the mental health programs and to become trained as a psychotherapist. I was attracted to the idea and at the same time, scared to make a change. My ruminations regarding what I should do went on and on ad nauseam. Back then, I knew nothing about dharma, spiritual journeys, or even good decision-making, yet somehow, I eventually said "Yes." This choice turned out to be a great gift because I learned the art of psychotherapy from very competent teachers.

This was the beginning of a long career as a therapist. I have never regretted this decision. Through it, I have served many people in their recoveries and transformations. Along the way, more doors opened to sacred dimensions. I learned to say "Yes" to other amazing pathways that explored the larger dimensions of our lives. By saying yes to the offer of training as a therapist, I found my true calling. My dharma for this lifetime is clear—to help others heal deep psychological and relationship wounds and to lead people forward on their spiritual journeys. Everyday Soul Dances *is one of the outgrowths of this initial choice and an offering to others to find their own inimitable journeys.*

What I have found over the years is that with the right kind of understanding and intentions, all actions become dharmic and sacred. In service to such intentions, a goal we might have is to increase our attention and awareness in the present moment more and more of the time. When we live less-conscious lives, we live in more automatic, addictive, and robotic ways just to get things done. This dulls our senses and limits our capabilities. As this happens, we often become resentful, depleted, depressed, addicted, unmotivated, and acting in ways that keep us apart from who we truly are.

When we pay attention in new ways, we make the right use of our talents and capabilities, and we give proper attention to our everyday acts. As a result, we become less stressed and calmer—more willing to engage with the tasks and people at hand. When our daily lives become more inspired, more easeful, and more loving, we feel a lightness of being, and we will enjoy our lives a lot more. We do what is right for us to do in the present moment, in all areas of our life, no matter what they are. We perform our daily tasks with an awareness that we are spiritual beings living sacred lives and know that we are touching the highest good by our very acts alone. This is grace, this is dharma, this is our divinity in action, and this, Dear One, becomes your daily Soul Dance.

CONTEMPLATION

What is your highest purpose in this lifetime as you know it today?

If you were to be in greater alignment with your soul's purpose, what would you do differently?

Whenever you are feeling stuck, ask yourself "How am I fulfilling my soul's purpose by _____?" Then write more about your answer. You might also revisit the previous questions in this chapter to stimulate ideas that will foster change.

Now bow down to yourself with your hands in prayer position, honoring yourself as you delve deeper into your dharma.

Namaste

CHAPTER 8

CREATING YOUR MOST SACRED DESTINY

My Most Beautiful Dear One,

As you more consciously create your sacred destiny, do not hold back. So much is at stake and so much is possible. There is much for you to embody, yet you have hesitancy and fear. New days are dawning for you. Please embrace this dance of your amazing life. Your soul knows the story of your destiny. You only must open to the possibilities and intricacies of who you are. Then you will find that the great beings are waiting for you and drawing you forward. This is the time for you to make a full commitment to your most sacred life, to access the potentials of your unique and vital soul's dance.

At times, it is easy for you to follow that which you love and to find the joys and miracles being created along the way. At other times, you may find yourself alone, broken, and in the dark. During these times, stay open to your feelings, to your questions, to your dreams, and your longings. When you hold back, you stay small and limited in possibilities. This is not who you truly are or who you want to be. As you increasingly remember that you are a spiritual being, you will long to experience this state in its fullest possibilities. It is time to take full responsibility and to accept and receive the support of all kinds available to you. Increasingly you want to experience these highest states again and again. Gradually you will learn and then remember how to make shifts in your consciousness and in your ways that bring you back home to your most sacred Self.

Always I uphold you, encourage you, and bless you. Remember that, from my vantage point, you are a beautiful being with unlimited potential. I see you as magnificent! Your talents, words, and ways are longing for expression. Your world needs what you have to offer. I am here to support your sacred adventures. A fuller life lies ahead. Come home to your highest possibilities. Say "YES!" There is complete support for you as you open and embrace who you are becoming. Remember who you are and join with Me once again.

Within each of you lies an ancient longing for wholeness and balance. I, the Divine Feminine, speak to you at this time to foster the need for integration and balance within each of you and within our broken world. This is the time of the return of the Goddess and a new and necessary blending of the Divine Masculine and the Divine Feminine. Within each of you, this communion will occur as you consciously create your most fulfilling life and learn to extend and expand your love towards everyone you touch and in each word that you speak. Your destiny is to be a bearer, a carrier of My lighted ways. And this, Dear One, is what will bring balance to your lives and what will heal your relationships with each other and our Earth.

Our past-accumulated karmas from previous lifetimes create our destiny in this life. Apparently, in-between times, our soul makes agreements about what ways and situations are necessary for soul growth in the next lifetime. Our destiny becomes the overarching principle for what we are to experience in that life.

We can understand destiny from the moment a child is conceived. Her destiny is based upon the circumstances of her life as it evolved from before the moment of conception. A child born in poverty and difficult circumstances, perhaps in a war-torn region, will have more disadvantages to overcome than a child born into a more affluent and peaceful region. This second child will be given more opportunities to develop her talents and be more readily able to become all she can be. Sometimes we hear heartwarming stories of children born in adverse conditions who were able to move beyond difficult circumstances and become great in their unique ways. Karma and destiny play many roles in determining who each of us is meant to be.

In contemplating how to write about destiny, I compiled a partial list of some of the ingredients of our human lives that have to do with our karma and that, in totality, create our destiny:

- our life circumstances such as where we were born and the opportunities, or lack of, we are given

- our past and current life experiences

- our genetics

- our neurobiology

- our ancestry and the countries and challenges that were present at the time of our birth

- our family dynamics – past and present

- how well we take care of ourselves in terms of diet, exercise, and rest or not

- our relationships – how well and how many people we love and how we handle difficulties in relationships

- our spirituality and religion

- our relationships to other beings and the Earth

- our psychological and physical well-being dis-eases

- our disorders such as addictions, anxiety, and depression

- our previous karma and karmic imprints that will be expressed in this life

- the ways we love, the ways we are broken by love, and the ways we open to deeper loving

- the geopolitical conditions of the world at the time of our lives

- our environment, the mores, values, and expectations of our culture and subcultures

- the karmas and destinies of family members and those in the communities in which we live

- those we meet during our lives who have a great impact on us, and their karmas and destinies.

You may have other details to add to this list. All this, and more, create our multifaceted selves— all unique, yet similar. Then, when we add others to the mix, with all their karma, dharma, and destinies, we truly have lives of cosmic complexity. When I think of who we are in our humanness, I am awed and humbled. Also, once we know and honor our humanness with its limitations and its immensities, it is much easier to drop all judgments of ourselves and others and to have great humility in the face of it all. No human mind could begin to fathom these multifaceted interweavings let alone set them all in motion. Truly, we all are actors on an exceptionally large and mind-bending cosmic stage. When we play our parts well, miracles occur within our lives, within the lives of other people, and within the weavings of universal design.

Your soul knows your destiny, at least in broad brush strokes. The challenge becomes a search for those specific pieces of the puzzle that become your life. This knowing comes from the sacred contract your soul made between lifetimes. Our greatest destiny is to manifest the ways of the soul as we journey back home to our most lighted Selves.

All that happens to each of us must happen for the healing and exultation of your soul's development. Some experiences were written into your soul's patterning and your destiny from the beginning of time. Others are choices we made along the way to learn what we need to learn in a particular lifetime. When we understand destiny, we can have a large hand in creating and fulfilling it. We become artists of our days. When our intentions are strong and clear and when we pay better attention to how we are living our lives, we will find the pathways that lead us forward to the discovery of the gifts that will show us more of the way. As we walk along these sacred pathways, we learn to embrace it all—the abject sorrows, the travesties, the impossible loving, and the magical, grace-filled states that surprise us beyond belief.

CONTEMPLATION

Write examples of karma, dharma, and destiny, as you understand them in your life.

In what ways are you growing spiritually and in all areas of your life?

What needs to be healed within you?

What are your next steps? And how will you fulfill them?

How will knowing about karma, dharma, and destiny help to show you the ways forward in your life?

PART IV

LIVING THE GREAT MYSTERY

CHAPTER 9

THE YOGA OF JUST ABOUT EVERYTHING

Yoga, quite simply, means union. In our society, we usually think of yoga as the practice of Hatha Yoga, the beautiful yogic form that brings us back into the awareness of our body, breath, and spirit. Other forms focus on love, service, and bringing oneself into communion with the Divine in all aspects of our daily lives. In a larger sense, yoga is a journey from one state to more enlightened ones of living in spiritual awareness in our relationships, in our personal growth, in our work lives, and throughout our lifetimes. It also is about what we learn along the way.

Once we begin exploring that which brings us into wholeness in any aspect of our lives, we learn to move from one state to another. This is easy to understand in the Hatha yoga asanas. One might follow a backbend with a forward bend and then end with Mountain Pose. The Mountain Pose grounds us into Mother Earth as we reach towards the heavens, standing in complete stillness and becoming One with All That Is. Similarly, we might follow times of our activities with time for journaling and contemplation as we always practice paying deeper and deeper attention to our state of being. This yogic journey helps us find our way home to our truer Selves and the realm of the Divine. This journey takes place over a lifetime as it brings us to a higher understanding of what it means to be human.

The union implicit in Yogic practices has various meanings to me. It is the union of mind, body, and spirit, and it is the communion we have in intimate relationships. It also is the union of the personal self with the Divine Self. All the practices of the various branches of yoga lead us forward into Oneness in all their various permutations.

Yoga is a vast homecoming for any of us who make the journey. There are steps along the way that we take to bring us more into harmony, balance, wisdom, and love. It is a way of embracing new ways and of letting go of old ones. And because we are delving into states of Divine Consciousness, these various practices become holy acts uniting us with our mystical nature. When this happens, veils covering our brilliance lift. Then we see with new eyes and open hearts as we enter grace-filled states. Each time this happens, we grow into ways of heightened fullness, greater wisdom, and amazing love.

Here is how it goes. In being human, we have at least two distinct parts to our evolution. Many of us may not know this until we begin our spiritual journey. First, we have our ego-self, which we develop during our early years and throughout our lifetimes. The ego is both our friend and our enemy. We need our egos to function successfully in the world, to establish our uniqueness, talents, abilities, and to interact with others; however, our egos also hold the karma we carry for this lifetime. Our egos are quite determined that their ways are the right and only ways. The ego must be in control, and, when it is not, it is threatened and will do whatever is necessary to reestablish control including creating great dramas and traumas, both emotional and physical, along the way. These methods to retain control are less than advantageous as they cause conflicts with others who also have their ego investments in how things are going. The results can lead to anger, victimization, depression, anxiety, and addictions, and they tend to get more and more out of hand, causing increasingly larger problems for the individuals involved and for those around them.

When we notice patterns that we do not particularly like about ourselves, we have many ways to receive help. Psychotherapy is particularly important on this journey as it helps us understand in deeper ways the dynamics in our families and the roles we played within our original families. We begin to recognize the damage created by family dysfunction and the ways we repetitively play out early family dynamics in our adult lives. With successful sessions of psychotherapy, there will be an emotional release of pain from past situations as well as from present ones. This kind of release allows us to experience a greater appreciation of others so that we are no longer bound up in the karmic patterns that held us back in such negative ways. With this experience of release comes a feeling of relief and a newfound sense of freedom. We begin to correct course with greater humility and a lessening of our old and habitual ego-based constructions.

Often it is in working through our psychological distortions and/or physical illnesses that there are openings to a spiritual longing and quests for something greater than the ways we have been living. This is because, in our pain, we need to break down the old defenses and search for relief, which implies changes in ways of being. This is when we start asking ourselves questions such as:

"Who am I?"
"What am I doing with my life?"
"Where am I going?"

We start realizing that life in the physical body only lasts for so long and that we want to live it more fully. We begin our spiritual journeys when we remember that we are spiritual beings and that there is so much more to our stories.

Many amazing and surprising adventures occur along the paths of such searching. There is a spiritual truism that states that when you do your part with intention and diligence, the universe will open to you in astonishing ways and show you the next steps to take as you ease into new ways of being.

The information that you are receiving and the practices that you will learn as you continue your *everyday soul dance* journey are moving you from an ego-based state to a being that is becoming more conscious, more aware, more centered, more relaxed, and more loving. Each step you are taking is a gift you give to yourself, one that keeps on bringing greater serenity and value to your most precious life. And, in the process of uniting with All That Is Sacred, you bring great gifts to others around you. In these ways, you are practicing a high form of yoga by uniting with All That Is.

CONTEMPLATION

Who am I?

Where am I going?

What are the next steps I need to take so that I move more fully into my Higher Self?

CHAPTER 10

INVITING SPIRITUAL QUALITIES INTO OUR DAILY LIVES

Spiritual qualities are those that assist us in maintaining high states of being as we live our daily lives. When we honor and abide by these qualities, they bring us home. While there are many such qualities, we will focus on four that hold great meaning for creating spiritual shifts. These qualities are Consecration, Constancy, Courage, and Contemplation. By consistently bringing our daily actions into harmony with these qualities, the very essence of our life changes. Perhaps you will find that you already are living some of these qualities in parts of your life. Please honor and celebrate all your current practices. When we pay closer attention to these qualities, we become more committed and more aware of all parts of our lives.

May these contemplations and practices bring about increased growth and understanding for you. May they lead to sacred experiences.

As we pay closer attention to how often we practice these important qualities, we naturally move into states of grace and gracefulness that bring us into greater harmony with our Higher Selves. Spiritual practices provide a grounding force during times when our life goes awry and becomes more difficult or even falls into chaos. They show how to shift our focus away from grief, despair, anger, and confusion.

These four qualities of Consecration, Constancy, Courage, and Contemplation are the underpinnings of any successful endeavor. With these qualities in place in our lives, we thrive in whatever we choose to do because we are acting in concert with the highest aspects of our being. In the case of our journey to our Higher Self, we consecrate our lives or specific parts of our lives to a path of spiritual growth. We stay true to that path with dedicated constancy as we continue each practice until the desired result is obtained. Along the way, it is easy to become derailed and fearful, especially as we enter new ways of being. So, we learn to practice courage. We become fearless because we believe in what we are doing, and we know that we have committed to something greater than our everyday selves. This commitment carries within it energies that support our growth and our return to wholeness. Because we have consecrated this part of our lives, we trust that there is sacred support for all that is involved. Finally, we contemplate what we are doing and how things are going, asking for help when it is needed and correcting course by making any necessary changes as we become aware of better and purer actions.

CHAPTER 11

CONSECRATION

To consecrate means to make sacred and to dedicate oneself to a higher purpose. Consecration is a sacred act that evokes a way of being at one with the Divine. It presupposes some sort of ritual, intention, and/or prayer to bring our lives into a stronger and deeper spiritual alignment. When I contemplate the word "Consecrate," I immediately remember my connection with the Divine. Then either my less significant acts of everyday life take a backseat for a while or I consecrate all the actions of my day to make them sacred through the right kinds of attention and actions. Each time we do so, we transport ourselves into an expanded vision of who we are as we connect to the sacred, to all other beings, and the Divine Mother herself. In living this way, we open to untold possibilities and clarity.

Any rituals that you care to establish will benefit you as you grow into higher consciousness and call forth the Divine. Perhaps you already have some in place. Music, prayer, Hatha yoga, Qi Gong, sacred dance, daily readings, and journaling are some uplifting examples to remind us of our sanctity and to center us in that sanctity. I will share a personal story with you of one of my own experiences of consecration.

My prayer for the writing of this book began many years ago when I received a clear inner message that I was to write a book called Everyday Soul Dances. *The specific words of the Divine Feminine that you have read here came to me early on. I was and am awed and inspired by them. I love Her messages. They are so very uplifting, true, loving, and encouraging. They became the beginning and end of this book.*

In writing this book, I contemplated deeply about how I was living my life. This contemplation happened over and over and has not stopped even as the writing of this book has come to its completion. Sometimes the writing ways were lost to times of illness. Sometimes other parts of living took precedence. Not too long ago my professional life shifted and that freed up more time for writing.

I created a beautiful peach-colored office in my home with a serene picture of Lake Tahoe on the far wall just beyond my computer screen. I have statues and pictures of the Goddess in some of her different aspects in this room. Before I sat down to write, I cleaned this room and removed all the bills and other life's "essentials" that could become distractions Then I lit a candle and incense and offered the writing time to Her.

My simple prayer was:

Please help me be a faithful guide so that it is Your words and ways that move through me. May I express them in the most evocative ways. May these words become a guide for others who will read them. I thank You for all that You have given to me so that I can serve You in this way.

I bowed down to my higher Self and the Mother of Us All with my hands in prayer position. I joined with Her and then opened to receiving Her wisdom and Her grace.

Namaste

When I got distracted, waylaid, and fearful—in other words, caught in my ego with messages like "Who do you think you are to write such a book?"—I would go for a walk, practice Hatha Yoga or Qi Gong. I would contemplate and meditate or write in my journal about what was going on. If I felt stuck on a particular subject, I studied more about it and then gave myself affirmations about taking the next steps. I reminded myself that writing this book was my dharma. And that never failed to get me back on track and ready to write again.

We can consecrate ourselves to anything important to our lives—a project, a creative act, healing that we need, or a way of being such as being a kinder partner or a better parent. Before you go to sleep at night, it is good to evaluate how your day has gone, then name your intention and prayer for this consecration for your next day. Such a practice opens your subconscious mind to ground your intentions. When you awaken in the morning, it is good to remember your prayer, intention, and consecration to make sacred all that you do in this new day. It is also good to be specific with your intentions, offering them as a prayer for the highest possible outcome. Then in the evening, note how it all went. What worked well? What needs course correction? These are great questions for your journaling. Writing a gratitude list for the unique events of this day provides an especially good ending for the day.

Take some time now to think about what you have read so far and how these words touch your life and how they honor all that you are, and perhaps questioning different aspects of how you are living. Please do not judge yourself. Instead, be open to new visions of the growing possibilities that you have always longed for.

CONTEMPLATION

Please honor all the ways you already consecrate your life.

Ask yourself "How do I consecrate this day, my work, my relationships, the roles I play?"

Write about these ways. This is your baseline. It is important.

If you have creative ideas that you have not made time for, write them down now.
On the other hand, you might have relationships that you want to improve. Write down these ideas, as they will be ways forward for you.

Write your Consecration to your Soul Dance as you know it today.
You may want to contemplate or pray. You might want to create a sacred space in your home, light a candle, and then think about what it means for you to consecrate your life to its highest purposes. Have your journal ready to write what is most true, inspirational, and vital for you. You might write a poem or create art – whatever is right for you each time you do this.

CHAPTER 12

CONSTANCY

I love to talk and write about Constancy with people who are stepping onto their spiritual path for the first time, with those who have been walking that path for a long time, or with those seekers who may have taken a detour off the path and are ready to get back on it. This is because constancy is the means to maintaining a consistent commitment to anything that we set out to do. In my own life, and my work with others as a psychotherapist and a coach, I have found that when we engage in any endeavor, one of the biggest obstacles we face is staying constant and loyal to ourselves and our intentions and commitments. When we give in to diversions or malaise, or when we start something and then just give up, we make little progress in terms of our goals. However, those who are successful in anything practice the principle of constancy to see the action through to its logical conclusion, whether it is getting a Ph.D., becoming skilled at baseball, changing eating habits, training for a marathon, or embarking upon a spiritual path. Constancy is the tool for fulfilling a commitment.

So how do you apply the principle of constancy to your spiritual journey? First, you choose a goal, something that you have been promising yourself that you would like to accomplish but have not. It does not have to be something complex. Starting with something simple to do each day is a wise choice. Commit to yourself that you will actively work toward your goal each day for 30 days. Staying the course every one of those 30 days is an act of constancy and helps you establish a new routine. At this point, I recommend adding additional days until day 90 of your daily practice is reached. By this time, you likely will have firmly established a regular daily practice, a "habit," meaning that you will be more likely to continue from that day onward. The rewards are obvious. You will feel inspired and will want to continue.

Constancy also is a state of being in which we hold to our spiritually, emotionally, and physically grounded center. We all have had times in our lives when emotions have overtaken us, when we have come undone, and when we have reacted in ways that we later wish we had not. When we fall apart, crises worsen, and we later may feel ashamed, embarrassed, and disappointed in ourselves.

So, as you practice the ways of these Soul Dances, you will have daily opportunities to practice constancy. See this practice as a challenge, as a fun adventure, and as an act of dedication to yourself and your greater Self. This practice of constancy is a core approach to becoming successful in what you aim to accomplish. Along the way, with this practice in place, you will find yourself becoming clearer about what you want and more assured as you walk these new paths. As you complete your challenge, you will experience greater enthusiasm, a renewed sense of strength, and a strong conviction that you can do anything you choose to do.

Of course, none of us will immediately take on all the challenges of each spiritual practice outlined in this book. Instead, look through each chapter and then select the one practice that is most important to you in your life right now or the one you like the most. Then commit to this practice, first for 30 days and then, ideally for 90 days. Along the way, contemplate your experiences, write about them, and share them with others.

Above all, I want you to be successful in walking this lighted path. I want each of you who are reading these words to feel more courageous, more connected to your Self and the Divine Feminine. I hope that along the way, you will be delighted in new expressions that develop in your life. Remember too that balance is important. Practice relaxing through your days with that same kind of constancy and dedication. Be thoughtful and have fun with the new ways. Please be gentle with yourself if you veer off the path. Inconstancy can happen for a variety of reasons, all of which have to do with the simple fact that we are human and that other parts of our lives can get in the way. When you recognize what has happened, get back on track. Then you can create a new beginning with renewed energy.

As you practice constancy over time, it becomes the mainstay of a consecrated life. The keyword here, of course, is practice, whether it is in its noun or verb form. We usually do not get instant results in any "practice" that requires us "to practice." All such changes take place with repeated practice throughout our lifetime. To gain the best fruits of anything we do, we keep on living in those ways that bring us home. Because we are reaching for the highest, we rarely are bored and, instead, we become invigorated. We find that the changes that come with constancy are so magical and strong that we joyfully embrace them as essential aspects of our lives.

Elaine Hoem

CONTEMPLATION

Spend some time contemplating the spiritual practice of constancy in your life. Write about successes that you have had as you practice something diligently over time.

Think of a time in your life where you got off the track in a commitment. Write about what happened and how you got back on.

What inner and outer resources do you need to be constant with a specific project?

What is your next step in using these resources?

CHAPTER 13

COURAGE

When we live in awareness, present moment consciousness, and loving connectedness with All That Is, we are living a life that is in alignment with our Higher Self, with our true destiny. With constancy in our practice, we can maintain this connection for an exceptionally long time. However, because we are human, we can still lose our way from time to time and fall into fearful and resistant places. When fear grabs us, we collapse into our smaller selves and we become anxious and contracted. We suffer, worry obsessively, and remain stuck in our old and now ineffective ways. It is difficult to be completely free of fear given all that is happening in our world today and in a human lifetime; yet we can practice maintaining higher states of consciousness so that when tragedies strike, we have the inner resources to do what needs to be done and to put our fears into the background of our minds.

Maintaining courage in our journey to fearlessness is the yogic dance that moves us beyond any fear and onto the road to our open hearts where we stand strong and act from our deepest wisdom. When our hearts are open, our good judgment expands; we are free to love deeply, to love many, and to love well. On the other side of the continuum, the fear-based side, we lose our courage, close down, and try to slink away into a hole for perceived protection. When we close our hearts and run away, we miss opportunities to grow spiritually, both personally and in relationship. Usually, we shut down when we are feeling the need to be self-protective or when we are just plain scared. These ways are not a surprise, and, in fact, we probably are remarkably familiar with them, as we have built these kinds of defenses over lifetimes. It is a part of our humanity to fall away and then to move forward again.

When we were children, our self-protective instincts may have been very appropriate because of a wounding we experienced when love was absent or too distorted. As we grow, these instincts become habitual, as they are the only way we know to cope with problems. The downside of regularly responding to uncomfortable situations with these less-conscious choices is that we remain stuck in questionable patterns that keep spiritual growth at bay. Our beautiful, loving hearts close, and deeper love becomes difficult or impossible to find. However, when we look at those habitual response patterns of fear, denial, retreat, or simply a general malaise straight on with honesty, we have opportunities to make shifts that bring us into more conscious and connected states.

Of all the patterned responses that keep us from moving forward, fear is often the most prevalent one. For reasons known or unknown, the fear of what we might find on the other side of depression, anxiety, or addiction, new decisions about jobs, a place to live, or the state of a relationship keeps us stuck in those old states and positions. If these responses are due to unexamined and unhealed trauma from past experiences of abuse or neglect in childhood or trauma in your current life, it may be time to sit down with a psychotherapist and process through the trauma until healing takes place. This is often an essential starting place, and always a vital one no matter where it enters the healing journey. However, if therapy such as this, or other healing practices, that would foster your growth are something that you have been aware of but continue to avoid, *Everyday Soul Dances'* words and contemplations will open doors to movement and courage for you.

As we begin to tap into our courage and look closely at our fears with the intent of overcoming them, one of the first things that we discover is that our biggest fear may be the fear of change. Often our fears come from ego-based states in which we feel that we need to be in control, and it is hard to maintain *any* control when we are facing change. The fact is, though, that we are always moving between states of numbness and discomfort, between confusion and anxiety into ways of aliveness, openness, creativity, strength, and trust. This is one of the dances of yoga. It is one of the patterns of our lives.

At the same time, it is important to keep in mind that being fearful is normal and even healthy at times such as when we are confronted with a physical threat or a severe psychological one. In such circumstances, our fear can help us ignite ways to protect ourselves and others. So please do not chastise yourself for feeling fearful. Fear becomes crippling only when we do not move beyond it and stay stuck in our smallness. Admitting to our fear is the very beginning of transforming fear into courage. The courage to overcome fear creates an essential new alignment with our spirit that allows us to join with our Higher Selves. New and larger energies support us and open us to fresh and grace-filled ways to handle fearful situations. And, when we look at our lives from a spiritual perspective, we understand that even fear-filled situations can be necessary for our soul's growth and that we have the means to learn from these experiences and then move beyond them.

Gathering our courage in hand to face and then relieve ourselves of the old, worn-out messages that keep us stuck allows us to become more potent than our fears. Once we name these new truths about ourselves and practice holding *them* in place instead of the old negative beliefs, we are better able to move beyond fear, because we have a new and often intriguing vision of what is possible. This is both a huge relief and a great gift. The newly developing lack of fear and the strength of courage change us significantly, as we make a leap of faith and step into new and more courageous ways of being. Doorways that we could not see before now begin to appear. Our newly discovered courage allows us to open some of these doors to discover what is on the other side. As we open ourselves to these new opportunities for self-discovery, free of our old fears, the beauty of our true selves begins to emerge.

When we go further into contemplating our fear and even further into contemplating our longing for a vision of who we can be, then we begin to open to change. Two good questions to contemplate are: *"If I stay the same what will happen?"* and *"If I make a shift, what might happen?"* To find those answers, we may do some research, or we may hear exactly the right words that point to a new way. We may meditate and receive an intuition about our next steps, or we may write about our fear.

The more open we become, the more opportunities we will have to seek and find new directions. When we honor these nudges by paying attention, we open to new and growth-filled possibilities.

Then we can take our next steps to return towards what we know to be true about ourselves. When these shifts occur, we are creating anew with bolder and more creative ways of living.

One of the beautiful lessons we learn from personal coaching is that of making changes in any area of our lives by taking small, doable steps. When it comes to fear, these small steps lead us to ever-widening pathways that open onto more courageous actions. Any new step, no matter how small, is a courageous one. Once we have defined exactly what these steps are, we naturally begin to reduce our levels of fear and anxiety to begin the journey that moves us towards more fulfilling and creative lives.

The following exercise is effective in delineating some steps you can take to reduce fear and move into greater clarity and greater courage.

WHAT I KNOW TO BE TRUE

Plan to do some writing in your journal. You will be addressing some specific truths of who you are. Through this writing, you will permit yourself to make shifts in your thinking and in how you live your life. You will also write clear and positive affirmations to strengthen your resolve to change some present beliefs. This is a powerful exercise. Please practice it whenever you are stuck.

Make yourself comfortable, sitting in a place that is quiet so that you can easily write. Do a bit of stretching and bending first to become aware of yourself in your body. Then breathe deeply and fully, centering yourself and grounding yourself deeply into the Earth.

As you breathe, breathe deeply from your belly, and relax as much as possible.

Take up your pen, pencil, or tablet and write your intention and your goal. What is your vision of the changes you would like to make? It may be a career shift. It may involve a relationship, or an intention to take better care of yourself.

Then ask yourself two questions: "What will happen if things continue in the same ways they are now?" and "What will happen if I make changes in alignment with my new vision?"

Write down both sets of answers.

Next, examine some of the beliefs that you have about change itself. A simple but effective way to do this is to write down statements that you know to be true.

Here are some examples:

It is okay to be afraid.

It is okay to move forward.

It is okay to fail.

It is okay to start again.

It is okay to move beyond messages about who I am that are not productive.

I have many wonderful qualities and strengths despite this current problem.

These qualities are: _____

_____

_____

_____

_____

The spiritual qualities that will help me move forward are:

_____

_____

_____

_____

I know how to work through difficult situations.

Then write about a recent example.

If I do not know enough to move the fearful energies, I will ask for help from _____

I know the joy and strength of coming out on the other side of fear.

I am learning.

I am resilient.

Even though I am scared, I will change my ways, act with courage, and move forward with my life.

~

I recommend writing as many truths about yourself as you can think of. Keep writing until you run out of ideas. This writing creates a new alignment and deeper permission to be who you truly are.

Then ask yourself "What are the highest next steps I will take?" Let the thoughts come without any effort on your part and write them down as they come.

Now ask your guides, the Divine Mother, angels, and other ascended masters who support you to guide you in these new ways. Open your crown chakra and imagine drawing light from the heavens down through this chakra, through your spinal column, and deep into the Earth. In this way, you are grounding and aligning with both heavenly and earthly energies that stabilize and strengthen you. Imagine holding this alignment within until courage takes the place of fear.

Now write some affirmations in the present tense. For example:

Now I can move forward with courage and grace.

I love myself enough to make this change.

I am practicing stating only positive messages to myself about myself.

I am becoming strong and courageous.

I am _____.

I am _____.

I am _____.

The last steps are to bow deeply to yourself in Namaste with your hands in prayer position and consecrate your actions by honoring yourself and your contemplation to move beyond fear and into courage.

Then bless and honor any others who are involved.

Now sit quietly in meditation, breathing out all the fearful beliefs until you sense that they are gone. Then imagine filling all the released places with the new energies coming into you as sparkling golden light. Breathe this light in from the heavens. Fill every cell of your body.

Stay with the fullness of these new energies for as long as you wish.

In the days ahead, practice your permissions and your affirmations. Continue to write other ideas that come to you. If you need another's support, ask for it.

You can practice this exercise at any time, revisiting it whenever you feel stuck again. When we "write" ourselves into new ways of being, we become less confused and fearful. We open more to our potential and our spiritual essence. Along the way, you will find that you also are opening your heart to all your life experiences so that you can deeply honor your experiences with others and with yourself. You will find that your beautiful, divine Self is both within and without.

There are other time-tested ways to work with any fears daily. When a feeling of fear arises in us, we want to take notice right away and shift that fear before it turns into full-blown anxiety. This is where our newly discovered relationship with courage comes in handy! When we institute any of the practices listed below, our minds can make the shifts from fearfulness to fearlessness.

Here are some ways that are helpful to step into states of courage:

- Breathe deeply and slowly from your belly for long enough period to notice shifts in your state.

- If possible, go outside and breathe in the qualities of nature.

- Meditate.

- Repeat your mantra.

- Talk with wise, calm friends and teachers.

- Remember to write about who you are beyond the fearful places.

- Write about the goodness, possibilities, and stabilizing forces at play in your world.

- Take some action to know that you are making a difference.

- Exercise and relax.

- Dance it out.

- Play.

- Remember that there are soul lessons you are learning as you move from fear to courage.

- Do any of the things that bring you peace, comfort, love, and joy.

- Limit your exposure to any negative media, people or situations that tend to enhance your fear.

Be mindful and take care of yourself in these ways. This is the act of love—the love of yourself. Added to this love are the gifts of love that come to all of us from the Divine. Together, this is what allows us to open to All That Is. Loving ways become a much more constant experience. And as so beautifully happens on the spiritual path, the more we open, the more shifts we make that have energetic effects rippling out to others and into the universe for the good of all.

CONTEMPLATION

Write your experiences of moving successfully beyond fear into fearlessness.

How can your experiences of being courageous in some areas of your life help you in other parts of your life?

What are your next steps to becoming fearless in more areas of your life? What kind of support do you need to do so?

CHAPTER 14

CONTEMPLATION

Looking deeply into the essence of our lives brings greater meaning and honor to our experience as human beings. Too often in our society, we rush headlong from one thing to another to do all that needs to be done. In the process, it is easy to miss opportunities for contemplation and reflection. Yet without reflection, too often our lives can seem mundane and ordinary, lacking richness and meaning. Without due consideration, we often overlook the full beauty of everything that occurs all around us every day.

Contemplation, for me, means paying closer and deeper attention to all that we are, all that we do, and all that takes place around us. Each time we contemplate the deeper meaning of any issue, we are searching for the highest truths within ourselves—the truths that define our spiritual Self. We can only find that place when we courageously lessen our ego's hold over our choices so that we can let go of our attempts to be in constant control of ourselves and of others. When we understand more of what a life lived in this kind of freedom is like, we naturally become more humble, more connected, and more in awe of our journey. Once we open to these more inspired states, we also loosen the hold that negative karma has on us. In this way, we change our destiny, and we create environments that soften life's impact not only for ourselves but also for those whose lives we touch. In truth, we become the artistic creator of our days.

Contemplation helps us connect the dots of our life's experiences. Through these connections, we more readily enter sacred realms, giving us a greater chance to act for the good of all. When we rush through our days without paying attention to each moment—this movement, this decision—we find ourselves caught in ego-based thinking, hyper-emotionality, and less conscious ways of being that may be destructive to ourselves and others. When we are less aware, it is easy to create chaos and to keep reliving worn-out behaviors that do not get us where we intend to go.

When we allow time for contemplation, we are walking the path to wholehearted participation in our lives. We are creating deeper grooves in our awareness of our interconnectedness with All That Is. Our often-felt sense of isolation and the corresponding "doer-ship" that attempts to soothe that feeling of aloneness decrease while our spiritual development opens and expands. Spiritual awareness changes everything—our perceptions, our beliefs, our choices of action. In place of a kind of dullness, we become more and more alive. Through contemplation, we find the sacred steps of our unique dances in this life, and we watch with amazement how perfectly these steps interweave with others who dance with us.

Contemplating our needs, desires, emotions, and patterns of behavior without self-judgment opens many doors into the Self. We pay better attention to our lives, our karma, our dharma, and our loving. This is the work of the Divine moving through our human form so that our minds are clear, our hearts more open, and our ways inspired. The transformation from our small, limited selves into our sacred Selves occurs when we become open to our spiritual essence. This is the work of this lifetime. This is the journey of the sacred path. It is one of the reasons that you are reading this book.

WRITING YOUR WAY HOME

A journaling practice is one of the best companions to bring along the way. It helps us keep track of our ever-growing awareness of the new sensations and experiences that arise as we continue along our spiritual path. It brings punctuation and poignancy to our observations. It makes clear what we are experiencing and allows for significant emotional release as we put any confused and distorted feelings on paper.

Ideally, journaling is a daily practice with no pre-arranged expectations of how much or how little to write. At least once a day, we commit to paper those aspects of our day that seem important—what we felt, how we acted, what touched us, and what we learned.

Often, we find ourselves needing to write about the negative aspects of our day, the parts that confused us, created anxiety, or left us feeling helpless. This writing helps to release and settle our emotions, bringing greater clarity to our minds. In this way, it helps us grow beyond whatever is causing us dissatisfaction, distress, anger, or shame. As we write, we more easily discover the patterns of emotions and behaviors that we learned that have kept us limited. Letting those patterns flow onto the paper and remain there rather than rattling around in our minds helps to ground us so that we can re-establish our center.

Journaling also allows us to name our intentions in black and white. Doing so strengthens our resolution to shift and change and move in desired directions. One easy way to initiate change is to write our intentions for the next day the evening before. This allows the subconscious mind to strengthen these intentions while we sleep. In the morning, we can review these same intentions before starting our day.

Writing allows us to capture the stunning beauty of a day, the conversations we had that created change, and the experiences that led to silence or wonderment and delight. As we journal, a poem or a prayer may form or a picture might come to mind, and each might find its way onto the page. Once we begin to unwrap ourselves from our stuck places through words and pictures, we become more than we previously were. Each time we sit and affirm our life through writing about it, we turn the ordinary into the sacred. This is exactly what we want to do more and more of the time.

There are even more gifts that we give to ourselves when we journal. Through journaling, we can receive messages from the challenged and challenging inner parts of ourselves—our lost child-self, that angry teenage self, the hidden shadow self. When we write, we may also receive messages from the Divine Mother and the ascended masters that remind us of the grace flowing around and through us because of their presence in our lives. We find words that give wholeness to the wiser person we are becoming. We write to capture and crystallize dreams and to dispel any confusion that some of our dreams have created, replacing that confusion with greater clarity. When we write about our grief and our losses, our fears, and our painful remembrances of things past, we are courageously giving these experiences depth and enhanced understanding. We are ushering out our pain, and our gratefulness for this act opens doorways to desired shifts within us. With all these gifts, we are much more likely to honor the next steps we take.

Sometimes, the next steps take us to places that are also difficult. We feel lost, afraid, or broken; we want and need to return to our center. With our daily practice of journaling, we have the perfect way to move through these newly experienced challenges. When this happens to me, I know that I can write and write uncensored, allowing tears to flow and words to form, writing until there is nothing more to say. By this time, I usually feel drained—like a limp noodle. When there are no more thoughts, nothing more to release, I often take this page or pages and burn them, offering up the words to a fire so that their energies transmute into smoke and ether. Afterward, I take a break in my day, to walk or ride my bike, or do other activities that actively cleanse my being of all that I wrote.

This second exercise of WHAT I KNOW TO BE TRUE can be used once you have completed releasing all you had to release. It leads to healing. Again, we write the words "What I Know to Be True" as the heading. Rather than focusing on the problems, this time we invite ourselves to remember who we are when we are living with a full perspective that includes Goddess Consciousness. These statements contain only positive qualities—our strengths, our knowledge of how to handle problems, and our capabilities to move beyond the situations that trouble us. This is a great practice for any time we are stuck.

WHAT I KNOW TO BE TRUE

Write statements and affirmations such as:

I know I will survive this because _____.

I am strong even though this has happened to me.

I continue to love and support myself even though this has happened.

The other is not my enemy and is worthy of my love even though this has happened.

I am learning_____through this experience.

I pray for _____for myself.

I pray for _____for the other person.

I will reach out to _____for added insight into this situation.

I am letting go of _____karma by working through this in new ways.

Keep writing a litany of what you know to be true over and over until there is no more to say. This practice of WHAT I KNOW TO BE TRUE is a great grounding exercise after an emotional release. We begin to reestablish trust in ourselves again and to see beyond the problem area. The gift of this writing is a shift of perspective into greater wholeness.

Elaine Hoem

CONTEMPLATION

If you already practice contemplation and journaling, write about what these practices bring to your life.

If you are new to these practices, how will you begin, and what value do you see in them?

Practice writing daily so that you begin to deepen your connections to your experiences. Please make plans to keep your writing confidential.

DREAMING YOUR WAY HOME

I love dream work. It is inner work at its best—at its most exciting and creative. However, we need to learn to interpret dream language as it has a mind of its own and seems nonsensical, weird, and of no consequence until its true understanding resonates with us. When we interpret the dream symbols, the dream opens subconscious messages that we miss during our daily lives. They show that there is more to the story than our conscious mind is absorbing. Dreamwork is a fun and rewarding way to go deeper into your interior world. It is well worth any effort you make to analyze your dreams. I encourage you to begin to use your dreams as your guides if you do not already do so.

Some say that dreams are our inner gurus or counselors. I agree.

Dream symbol books can be beneficial guides; however, not all interpretations of dream symbols are true for everyone. They may or may not apply to your dream images so you will want to work with your images in ways that speak to your dream.

The following Dream Analysis is my favorite way to analyze dreams.

DREAM ANALYSIS

- Have a notebook and pen by your bed.

- Before falling asleep, ask or pray that your dream body opens to you during sleep and that you remember your dreams.

- When you awaken with a dream, do not move until you recall it in its entirety. Movement results in the loss of the dream memories.

- Recall the dream in as much detail as you can as if you are watching a movie.

- Keep the language in the present tense, i.e., "I am driving down a windy road in a fast red convertible".

* Then write the dream in your journal with these details again in the present tense.

* Think about any possible event in the past 24 hours that relates to the content of the dream; write about this waking event, asking yourself how it corresponds to the dream.

TO INTERPRET YOUR DREAM

* Take each symbol as a part of you and give each symbol a voice as if you are speaking for that part of yourself.

* There are often many symbols in a dream; they are all well-worth exploring and interpreting as they all give glimpses of parts of ourselves that are present in the dream yet not as available to us in waking life.

* Give your dream self a voice.

* What is the symbol that transforms, lights up, shows an expanded way, and teaches a lesson for your waking life?

* After compiling all the messages from each symbol, you most likely will have an idea, or several ideas, about the dream and its larger messages to you; put them all together and write all this in your journal.

What have you learned? How do you feel once you have interpreted your dream? Where do you go from here based upon this dream? Are there specific actions in your waking life that would be good for you to take? Take some time to write the answers to these questions in your journal.

Disturbing dreams and nightmares are often difficult to transcend. As soon as you awaken from a dream of this nature and are aware enough to know that you have been dreaming, you can change the story as completely as you would like. To do so, find the place in the dream in which things start to go awry and redo your dream in your thoughts. Create a new story—one in which the disturbing parts no longer happen; instead, in this waking dream, you empower yourself to take control and to somehow banish the negative, dark, or scary parts. Make your waking dream self as powerful as you like. Become a superhero with epic capabilities to show that you are competent to shift these energies and that you are in control.

You may decide to move from the place of the frightened child into a version of yourself standing tall and strong, saying clearly and directly to the scary image before you that from here on out, you are in charge and that this image must leave—that it is diminished into nothingness and being sent into the stratosphere. As you do this, breathe deeply, and access your inner resources. If your child self is involved, take her in your arms, reassure her, and bring her into a more lighted place.

Now reassess the dream. Ask yourself how you are feeling now. Throughout the day, you can continue to stand in your power, using affirmations such as:

"_____no longer has the power to scare me. I am free and able to handle traumatizing thoughts and scary dream images."

"I now create only good in my life despite what happened in the dream or the past."

If you have been a victim of any sort, or suffer from PTSD, then these nightmares can be terrifying, and you might not feel ready to handle such images on your own. With such trauma in your past, trying to carry it by yourself can create even more fear and inability to cope. In this case, it would be good to have the assistance of a compassionate therapist who values dreamwork and who can help you with the dream experiences and other traumatic symptoms. Asking for help is always a courageous and self-loving thing to do.

In addition to analyzing your dreams and giving a conversational voice to each part, there are many other avenues of dream interpretation that you might explore. You can draw or paint the dream and its symbols. A poem might form. You may want to dance parts of the dream into wholeness. Consider making a list of how the dream characters represent parts of you. Then ask what would happen if you brought the qualities of these images more fully into your waking life. When we access the positive qualities, power, and messages from the dream images, we change. Our worldview becomes clearer. We stand stronger in our sense of ourselves, and we make course corrections as needed. All these ways encourage the deepening of communion with these newly revealed parts of you. In this way, the dream moves you from one state to another, into the direction you want to go.

You will know if your analysis of a dream has helped you with clearing some blockage in your emotions, psyche, or life. Often, we have an "aha" moment, a letting go. A clear understanding brings new information to us, an emotional release, an intuition, or a new direction to pursue. Sometimes, we have direct messages from a dream guide. At other times, our being relaxes when we release some old pattern. Sometimes a body symptom will suddenly be gone. All these ways and others that you may discover are signs that you have analyzed your dream correctly. This is the magic brought to you from your dream world.

At times, you may have to live with the dream images for a while until the messages have settled within and a new understanding is in place. One way to accomplish this is to deliberately go back into the dream in a meditative state and continue the dream dialogue in as much detail as possible. You might want to change a dream pattern so that you become clearer and more powerful instead of having the disturbing or frightening images retain their power over you. You might continue a dream to have it feel more complete. You might even want to change it completely until there is a deeper resonance with the truth of who you are.

Sometimes you will have a second or third dream during the same night's sleep that relates to the one you chose to analyze. Usually, these dreams, while seemingly quite different, will share common themes with the first one. Having their story enhances your ability to understand the underlying message.

Below are two dreams analyzed in a format that I find useful.

This dream is a dream a dreamer related to me for analysis. She is talking in the first-person voice as is recommended for recounting a dream.

The dream:

I am driving a classic sports car. It is sleek, red, and fast. It is an attention grabber, and it is mine. I am going speeding around a curvy mountainous road. I am thrilled and excited. The wind is tossing my hair and I have not a care in the world.

The Analysis of the Dream gives a voice for each symbol—in this case, the car, the road, and the dreamer.

The voice of the car:

I am an old, red, well-maintained, and beautiful sports car that belongs to the dreamer. She loves to drive me, and most of the time, I like the experiences as well. However, today she is going too fast for the mountainous road we are on. She is out of balance and into an old way of being. In the olden days, she thought she was Superwoman and that she could do things that were beyond what common sense and safety required. She has worked on this pattern over the years, but here she is again, caught in something dangerous and not true to her soulful Self. If she does not get a grip, we are going to crash and burn. I am in this dream to show her that her old ways, developed in the 70s and earlier, are untrue to who she is. I want her to be safe, self-reflective, and honoring of her experiences. In other words, she needs to slow down and pay attention to enjoy this amazing experience we are having right now. Because she is driving too fast, she is missing the true richness of this experience, which is sufficient and wonderful as it is.

The voice of the road:

I am a narrow mountainous road that goes from one state to another. The driver is aware of the dangers, twists, and turns that are a part of me. I run through majestic mountains, pine trees, light, and shadows. I am a metaphor for her to show her how she is living her life. Currently, it is not an easy journey. Excessive speed and lack of awareness are anathemas for her. She has committed to driving [i.e., walking] a spiritual path. Attention, intention, care, and ease are required to meet the challenges that the road and I represent. The old ways of unconsciousness and a sense of invincibility no longer work. These are limiting ways, ways of her ego. In fact, without the right attention and intention in this instance, she is likely to be in an accident, perhaps injuring others and even dying. If she stays true to who she is, she will remember that she travels all roads with an awareness that leads to humility and gratitude for all the challenges and opportunities presented. If a situation requires it, she attends to the present moment with caution and always with regard for all that is happening within and around her. In doing so, the gifts of this journey will come to her through all her senses, enriching her daily life. Such experiences are for her growth and her progress on her spiritual journey.

The voice of the dreamer:

I am the dreamer. The words of my car are correct. The cautions from the road are strong and true. I have been off base for the past day or so. I am not sure why, but I am rushing around, forgetting to breathe, and feeling a sense of self-importance and doer-ship. This old, lifelong habit is rarely present these days. I am revved up and too excited, feeling invincible; but this feeling is also uncomfortable, anxiety-based, and not healthy or safe for me. I need to shift gears downward to live in more conscious ways that honor the car's capabilities and the beauty of the scenery around me. In doing so, this experience becomes a grace-filled one in which I am at ease, in awe, and honoring All That Is during this time.

The transforming symbol:

The dreamer's voice:

What grabs my attention in this dream is "the road that goes from one state to another." This is movement from the ego state and its less-conscious ways to the more lighted state in which I connect with myself and with all that is around me. The way will be an enlightened one or not. It is my choice.

The lessons of this dream are:

Get back on track with a more soulful and less rushed connection to my life.

Slow down so that I can remember who I am in the present.

I can appreciate the car and the road, i.e., the gifts and lessons from the past and the present, but I do not have to live in old and unconscious ways.

Breathe!!!

Repeat my mantra when I am doing anything and everything. It is easy to do while driving. Then I pay much better attention to my driving and enjoy all that is around me.

Remember my commitment to the spiritual path.

Take in all that my life has to offer in this present moment—the experience of driving a great car, the stunning mountain road, and my connectedness with All That Is in any given moment or activity.

In my daily life, appreciate the people I encounter, the experiences I have, and the beauty and goodness of all life running through me and around me.

~

This dream is a simple one, yet its ramifications are large. If the dreamer pays attention, she will return to a quiet and thoughtful place in which her connections to her surroundings and herself are deep. She will live in open and serene states as often as possible. If she does not pay attention, however, she knows that she will receive other messages, possibly from other dreams, from others, or from actual life situations that will force her into awareness in less gentle ways. We are here to learn, so for this dreamer, it would be unwise to ignore such messages when the Compassionate One sends them to point her in directions that lead to growth.

Here is a second more complex dream experienced by the same dreamer.

The dream in the voice of the dreamer:

I have inherited a large house that I have not seen before. A happy family of four from Cape Town currently inhabits this house. They are vacationing in this area and are thrilled with all it has to offer. They thank me and get ready to leave.

I look around this place. It has large rooms filled with the previous owners' "stuff," paperwork so old that the edges are browning, furniture that has seen much better days, and walls that are crumbling. It is in a beautiful neighborhood and potentially could be a great home. Before that can happen, however, there is a huge amount of work to be done—getting rid of the former owners' leftovers, repairing, and replacing walls and appliances, painting, and opening dark spaces to bring in more light.

I know how to remodel homes. My mind goes to work immediately and creates a prioritized list of all that needs doing. One of the people with me has helped with previous remodeling projects, so I call him over, knowing that his work on this project will be stellar. Then I am on to other things with plans in place to undo, tear out the old, bring in light, and create beauty worthy of this house.

The Dream Analysis:

The voice of the family from Cape Town:

We are from far away, which means that we have expanded vision about this situation. Yes, the house is a mess; it needs lots of work, care, and redoing. There is more to the story. We are here to show the dreamer how people can be happy in this house. The fact that it is in disarray does not alarm us at all because we are enjoying the magnificence of the surrounding area. We see beyond the deficits and we are grateful for the opportunity to be here. We encourage her to take the same farsighted approach so that her way to clearing all this karma will be of the light.

<u>The voice of the house</u>:

I am all about old karma built up through generations and left for someone else to take care of. All of this is the lifework of the dreamer's ancestors that they left undone or incomplete. She has agreed to clear away as much of her family's karma as is possible in this lifetime. She has been doing this for years, and now, here is another piece for her to tackle. I know that she can and will do this. She is looking forward to the day in which all this is finished so that the gracefulness and beauty that is her potential will be evident. She tells me that she is longing for this clearing so that she can bring in more of the light, beauty, and elegance that is reflective of all she can become.

<u>The voice of the dreamer</u>:

This dream message is clear. It is simple to make shifts during my days to breathe, to be more conscious and present, to take care of all that I do, and to remember that I am practicing letting go of old, self-destructive ways.

It is very apparent to me that I am to let go of all these old, dark, dank, and useless trappings. Old ancestral beliefs, ways of being, pain, and sorrow have accumulated in my family, in this place for generations. I have inherited it all. It is part of my DNA, my ancestral memories, and the difficult karma with which I was raised. All the unwanted accumulation in this house is a metaphor for what needs to be cleared karmically. My dharma throughout my adult life is to see, heal, and release as much karma as possible. I need to clear lifetimes of darker, unresolved agendas that have kept my family of origin and me stuck and depressed. I know how to do this, both in remodeling houses and transforming psyches. I am good at such work and willingly tackle this project. It is the next step. I will have great satisfaction in accomplishing all that needs doing. I know I will love the finished project that will be beautiful, graceful, colorful, pure, and filled with love.

The transforming symbols:

In this dream, there are four symbols:

The family reminds the dreamer to see the bigger picture and to move beyond old, destructive ways in all the cleanup work.

Her challenge is to stay centered despite all the old karma she will be releasing. In other words, she will learn to see such work as sacred rather than as drudgery.

She is confident that she has the capability and skills to do this kind of work. She is clear, strong, and empowered.

Within the dream, she recognizes that she has another person and, in fact, an entire community that she can count on to help with this project. This demonstrates past progress in healing since in her waking life, she does indeed have healers, teachers, friends, and guides who have helped her clear karma that has been gnarly and difficult to clear on her own. Therefore, she knows that all this karmic clearing will result in a space that is pure, true, and beautiful.

The lessons of this dream, in her voice, are:

I am clearing more family karma.

I have the inner and outer resources to do this work even though there is a lot to do, and some of the clearing out is not easy, pleasant, or fun.

I trust, when all this work has been completed, the house will be beautiful and free and clear of the old and the dark. Once the darkness and the unwanted remains disappear and the remodeling, i.e., the healing, is in place, this home will be open to amazing light and the natural beauty surrounding it.

I do not have to do it all myself. I have good friends and competent people who are a part of my community who will help. We all have roles to play.

The dreamer and I analyzed this dream together. What occurred to her later demonstrates the value of dreamwork being so effective that it can have immediate and profound results. Within hours after analyzing this dream, the dreamer reported that there were shifts in her waking life. She experienced a lightness of being that manifested as a relaxation of tension that she had not known she was carrying. A problem with sinusitis that had suddenly come upon her during the night of the dream disappeared completely. On subsequent nights, she had other house remodeling dreams. Analyzing them showed that they too were about karmic conditions, but these dreams were about karma that she had created in this lifetime. They also needed clearing, in this case by bringing more inner work to a conscious level where she could dialogue with her younger self at various ages to give expression to the feelings of shame, guilt, despair, and a lack of forgiveness that she was harboring. Then, lovingly, and compassionately, she spoke with her younger self at each of those ages, blessing each one with the wisdom, forgiveness, and understanding that she had learned to acknowledge within herself as an adult. As a result, she was able to breathe out the wounding that had been locked in those parts of her. Only then was she able to fill those younger parts of herself with the radiant light of self-forgiveness and divine understanding.

The actual work of deconstruction and reconstruction of a home is not always easy or predictable, but it is necessary to complete to have a new room or home that is orderly and easy to maintain. Deconstructing our dreams and then constructing their messages also takes time and effort that is well spent. Our attention will result in information that will help break through the karmic blockages that keep us from being all we can be in the light of our Sacred Self.

CONTEMPLATION

Now it is your turn.

When you go to sleep and become aware that you are dreaming, write down your dreams and interpret them.

What are your new understandings based upon the dream interpretation?

Write down what changes you will make based upon information from your dreams.

CHAPTER 15

HONORING YOUR BODY TEMPLE

In our society, we learn early in our lives that our body is either beautiful or flawed. From a young age, girls especially are trained to model themselves after bodies that are the most beautiful, the thinnest, and seemingly the most attractive to others. We are perfect at finding faults with our bodies and our body parts. Our egos are hard at work when we find such fault. This way of identifying with our bodies can cause grief, depression, anxiety, and eating disorders. Even those who do meet the societal standards of beauty may suffer. Girls and women frequently learn to become sexual objects to attract and manipulate men. These efforts often come at the expense of true knowledge of the glorious Self within. Such patterns can well be at the expense of creating true, intimate, and loving relationships.

Boys, too, learn to judge themselves by societal standards of male beauty that either displease or please them. Having a muscular body is prized over a less muscularly developed one. "Locker room" mentality becomes an expected part of the everyday lives of boys of all ages. In this distorted subculture, many boys learn to see girls and women as objects for male pleasure and often little else. With a focus only on external beauty and how sexually pleasing this surface beauty is, misogyny is born. Girls and women may be abused or raped, and pornography runs rampant. This degradation of the body then sets in motion tremendous problems and expectations between men and women. Misogyny creates a false subculture. Then we wonder why all involved lose their way, and why relationship issues are rampant. When we live with distortions regarding our bodies, we can stay stuck in ways that are unrealistic, lacking in intimacy, and most definitely lacking in love.

A vastly different way of experiencing the body opens for people who embrace a spiritual path. The yogic traditions honor a much more expanded, compassionate, and vital way of being within the body. Quite simply, in yoga, the body is our sacred temple. It houses, informs, and protects our sacred Selves. Once we know that the Divine resides within, we begin to understand and honor the divinity that exists within each of us and each body, exactly as it is. The body is a storehouse of cosmic energies and karmic impressions that express themselves in both lighted ways and darkened shadows, yet each has immense capacities for transformation and love. But even beyond this realization is the fact that our bodies, minds, emotions, and souls are not separate entities. We are, in fact, one glorious whole, replete with Divine Consciousness. Once we have the understanding that this is so, we can experience, in potentiality, the communion with the Divine in which we can continually develop a new awareness about our whole Selves and our sacred purpose as we live our daily lives.

We continually remake ourselves by everything we do or neglect to do—every communication we have or do not have, the exercising we do or do not do, what we learn or ignore, how we take responsibility for our lives or fail in doing so, our nutrition, our meditations, our breathing, our thoughts, and even our rest. As yogis and yoginis, we learn to honor our body and our body temple to attend consciously to that which enhances rather than what deflects or defeats. We choose to become aware and careful in all that we do. When we choose to pay attention, a lifetime of learning can go into this deep honoring and care of the body.

The yogic traditions are replete with ancient information about how the sacred energies reside in the realm of the heart and in the energetic channel running along the spine called the Sushumna Nadi.[6] This channel holds and carries the energetic karmic impressions that have accumulated over our lifetimes. It most beautifully allows the universal life force, also called the Goddess Kundalini Shakti energies, to travel from the base of the spine to the crown of the head as spiritual awakening is taking place, usually with the help of a guru or enlightened teacher. Along the way, the chakras, or energy centers, within this column energize so that negative karmic holding patterns in the physical, subtle, and emotional bodies are released. Any such work is transformative and necessary for soul development. Once the negative karmic imprints are carried into this lifetime release, that piece of karma is over.

The yogic practices of Hatha yoga, chanting, and meditation both cleanse and open us to these energies. Along the way, we may become healthier and our thinking clearer. Creative ways may burst forth. Various mystical experiences may take place. These experiences are of the highest order, with transformation and blessings given as the result of the release of karmic distortions. These clearings happen as a necessary part of the spiritual journey. They are beyond the control of our minds, and they are much larger and greater than we can imagine. All these practices are wonderful to experience, oftentimes fun, and always good for our bodies and souls.

According to Barbara Brennan, an energy healer and founder of the Barbara Brennan School of Healing,[7] the energetic body extends out at least nine feet in all directions beyond our physical bodies. According to her expanded vision, we have several "sheaths," or layers, within our auric field. We may find impressions of wounding held within any of these energetic layers within both the physical and subtle bodies. A healer energetically removes such patterning so that healing takes place. Then we become freer from old wounding and negative karmas than we were before. Significant parts of our spiritual journeys have to do with the release of these negative energetic patterns to be free to open more to our Divine natures.

Barbara Brennan's book *Hands of Light* [8] depicts beautiful illustrations of the energetic layers beyond the physical body. These illustrations show who we are as lighted spiritual beings and some of the kinds of distortions that evolve from any wounding and trauma that we carry within our energetic bodies. Once negative energetic holding patterns release, our physical and emotional bodies can also heal.

Understanding our energetic bodies helps explain how easily we can connect with others since, from that perspective, we are sharing energetic space whenever we are in each other's presence. It is through the conscious use of the universal consciousness or the Kundalini Shakti that we can heal ourselves and others. Once we know, at the deepest levels of our being, that we are golden, lighted beings, that the Divine resides within us, that we all have imperfections, and that we all can heal ourselves and each other, we stand in humility and awe at the golden majesty and magnificence of the body temple. Then we are freer to practice living our lives in concert with the Spirit that resides within.

This Soul Dance moves us from a sense of smallness, limitations, and self-denigration to an expanded vision of ourselves and of humanity as a whole. In this expanded state, we unite with Divine Consciousness and with all beings. This is love. It is brilliant, stunning, and amazingly beautiful. These energies are so necessary to access during times in which our world seems so broken.

When we open to the energies of the Divine in all its forms, we find that these energies move within, through us, and around each of us into the farthest reaches of the cosmos. We start with an invitation—a calling to Her or from Her. We sit in silence to feel Her energies coursing through our being, and we learn to listen to Her messages that show us the way. Then, by living our life with Her as our Divine Partner, Muse, or Mother, our life is informed and transformed by Her loving and inspired thoughts. We understand, in ever-deepening ways, that our body is Her vessel, worthy of tender care.

When we honor our body as a temple that houses the Divine Spirit, which is our spiritual essence, there is a relaxation, a rhythm, and a resolve to care for it every day. This care becomes easier and more enjoyable over time. Hatha yoga practices help us find that care. As we hold the postures and move from one to the other, our body becomes amazingly and magically fluid and flexible. This fluidity and flexibility then extend to our emotions and our minds. We become calm; our minds become clear. We open to new possibilities and find that daily, we are honoring our Goddess Selves and our body temples. We live with minds and hearts that are open and more loving. The centeredness that we attain through these new attributes can carry through this lifetime and such a quiet state will inform who we are in future ones. Hatha Yoga is an ancient gateway to the Divine that naturally leads us into meditation. These ways are golden. When we find ourselves being clearer, stronger, more compassionate, more loving, fierier when necessary, and more passionate in all our ways, we will know, without a doubt, that it is Her infinite soulfulness that moves through us for the greater healing of ourselves and all others whose lives we touch.

If we have a body disorder, we may be able to heal a lot of it, and perhaps all of it, through good nutrition, the practices of Hatha yoga or other body-centered practices such as Qi Gong, or other exercises that are appropriate for our body type. Time spent with psychotherapists and hypnotherapists who can connect the past to the present, and the emotions to the body, also leads to new understanding and energetic shifts so that our body/mind/emotion triad can release what it is holding. Sometimes it is obvious that a healing has taken place; other times the experience is more subtle. One day you may wake up to discover that you are calmer and freer than you were before. This always seems like a miracle and it is. Such changes are indicative of the Goddess as she lives and moves within us. The Divine Feminine is anything but rigid. She wants us to laugh, to dance, to be sensual and sexual, and to have ecstatic experiences of communion with Her and with our loving partners. She is supremely free. Her gifts of freedom, sensuality, and sexuality come to us for our pleasure, for our expanded sense of self, and our loving communion with others.

If you hold less than constructive messages about your body, the following is an exercise that is beneficial to begin to release the negative beliefs. You can write a thank-you letter to your body and/ or to the body part that is troubling you. This letter will have only positive messages.

Here is an example of what you might want to write:

Dear Body,

Thank you for being a vital part of me this entire life. I thank you for holding me together all these years, for being so strong despite the times I have not treated you well. I value you, love you, and support you. I am incredibly grateful to you for your constant functioning.

I am learning to find the best ways to take care of you. I intend that you strengthen and heal so that you and I may be well. Then we can honor all the beauty and magnificence that is available for us to experience in this life. I commit to taking better care of you and my whole being. I honor you. You are amazing despite my less than thoughtful care. You keep functioning no matter what. You serve me well. I now see you as free of disease and other problems. Therefore, I am asking that all my organs learn to communicate more fully with each other so that there is greater congruence, cooperation, and heightened functioning amongst all my body systems. I also intend that you will relax more. I see you healed. I see my body, mind, and emotions healed so that we all attain a beautiful harmony that brings wisdom and deep peace. I see myself letting go of old karma and family dynamics that have kept us bound together in unhealthy states. I pray for perfect healing, for the answers we need to arise, and for the methods of healing to be made clear. I ask that the highest possible outcome become manifest. I always will search for healing answers. I commit to doing my part in more conscious and healthier ways.

I do honor you and I am always grateful.

Namaste

Any time you feel stuck and disparaging about the condition of your body, please spend some time writing in these ways to shift negative feelings and to allow healing to take place.

So how do we get from here to there?

First, in a very practical sense, we assess how well we care for our bodies in terms of exercise, food, relaxation, and play. Then we focus on specific methods of enhancing who we are through the conscious use of the breath, meditation, and active body exercises that put us in touch with Spirit. We also add practices that honor our sacred hearts and tame our minds. All these practices bring us more fully into our bodies and into who we are as we connect with Spirit.

CONTEMPLATION

Here are some questions for you. Please look at the answers without self-judgment. This is an exploration to bring you more into alignment with your beautiful body temple, just as it is and just as you would like it to be.

How well do I care for my body? If there are changes you would like to make, write them down in order of importance.

What needs healing?

Think about exercises that would enliven you and bring you joy, even if you have not tried them before. Think beyond the usual. Think Hatha yoga, Qi Gong, and dance to bring you closer to Spirit. Then, if you are ready, begin such a practice and notice what changes within.

Write about these changes.

What will you do to honor your body as Her temple?

CHAPTER 16

BREATHE... YOUR BREATH, YOUR PRANA, YOUR LIFE FORCE

Each breath we take is a part of All That Is. Remember that all energies are Her creation in both their smallest and infinite ways. The universal life force courses through us always, from our first to our last breath. In yogic traditions, this most essential and vital energy that connects us with all others, to our earth, and our universe is called Prana. Prana is our life force riding on the waves of our breath, sustaining life within us and permeating throughout the universe. Our prana is the bridge between body, mind, and spirit, and between life and death. It moves within us as our breath. When we live with lesser consciousness, we take our breath for granted and mostly ignore it. With awareness, we honor our breath and attend to it to bring more life force into our bodies, to help us clear our minds, to energize and realign our bodies, and to sustain thought-free states. With intention, we also can use our inhalations to enhance this energy for healing and our exhalations to remove toxins. We can use our breath to relax and to heal our bodies, minds, and emotions. When we use our breath as a part of our prayers, our yoga, and other spiritual practices, we strengthen our life force. Thus, we can send the energies to others for healing, and the healing of our even wider world. Conscious use of our breath leads us into meditation.

Once we know that Divinity resides within us, we pay more attention, both to our bodies and to our breath. Our breath is our constant companion. When used with awareness, it is a means of bringing us directly home to our sacred selves, immediately, joyfully, and powerfully. As we join with this expanded state, we grow into a truer version of ourselves. With conscious use of our breath, we can change our state from an anxious, confused, and scattered one into one of calmness and peace.

The breath is a bridge between our mind and our spirit. In and of itself, it is one of the aspects of the Divine. We breathe out what is ready to be released at all levels of our being and we breathe in the light, the grace, and the wonder of who we are in communion with the One. As we keep breathing with awareness, we realize that we can exhale smaller thoughts and worries, and breathe in All That Is, the I AM. After a time, we may find that the I AM presence is breathing us. Breathing then becomes a communion between each of us and the Divine. A conscious breathing practice brings us home to our inner Selves. It relaxes, heals, decreases anxiety, and opens us to our inner sacred states.

In my work with people who have problems with anxiety, one of the best practices I can offer is to teach relaxation techniques and breath awareness. When we practice deep yogic breathing, we cannot be anxious. It is impossible. Anxiety, in part, comes from shallow breathing in the upper, smaller third portion of our lungs. A full yogic breath uses the totality of our lungs and deeply relaxes, bringing us into greater harmony and expansiveness so that we find calmness and centeredness within ourselves. This breath is both simple and natural. As we practice conscious breathing with constancy, over time we create a more golden body vessel to receive, hold, and expand our consciousness. With intuition and intention, we use our Prana as an infinite power to change our lives. At the physiological level, when we breathe in this deep way, we oxygenate all the cells of the body. This allows for greater vitality and greater healing.

THE YOGIC BREATH

The yogic breath is a foundational practice on the spiritual path. Through this practice alone, we can naturally flow into meditation. It is easy, natural, and always occurring once we start paying attention.

First, place your hands on your belly. Then notice your lungs. Imagine them to be like two large balloons that are filling with air and then releasing. As we inhale fully, we naturally fill the bottom of the lungs, then the middle third behind the rib cage, and then to the smallest top third of the lungs.

Next, exhale completely allowing the breath to release from the top to the middle to the bottom.

That is it. As you move the air in and out from your belly, you will find your hands gently moving up as your belly fills with air and then releasing down on your exhalation. When this happens, you are breathing correctly. The breath you are practicing now is the same that you naturally breathed as a baby. Go back to this breath for a few minutes, breathing deeply and slowly and allowing your mind to be empty until you fall into a more relaxed state.

Repeat these breathing movements again and again. Start with 5 to 10 minutes and then slowly increase the time. After such practice, it is good to return gradually and gently to other parts of your life asking yourself "What do I need right now to honor these quieting shifts?"

If you have sleep problems or are emotionally upset, focus on conscious, slow, and relaxed breathing. If your mind is too active to relax, repeat a litany of relaxing words on each exhalation. Then with each repetition, allow your breathing to soften and move more slowly through you.

You can repeat the following words with every exhalation. At the same time, imagine your entire body relaxing with each word and exhalation:

rest...
relax...
restore...
revitalize...
heal...
soothe...
calm...
deep sleep...
deep sleep...
deep sleep...

Another powerful, healing breath exercise is to imagine the Infinite Source of Grace-Filled Light that is always moving through you and all around you in 360 degrees. As you inhale, breathe in this light, asking that it fill your entire body down to the cellular level. As you exhale, ask that you breathe out any toxins, blockages, or dis-ease that is ready to be released.

As you play with your breath and soothing words in these ways, your body is relaxing. Through physical relaxation, you are calming your mind and emotions and you are releasing tensions and blockages of energy. In this way, each time you pay attention, you are becoming a light-filled being. In this lightness of being, you enter the resting arms of the Mother and become united with Her.

Practice these breathing techniques often and especially during times when you notice that your breathing is shallow or during times that you are stressed. This is something you can do in most situations except when your full attention needs to be on an activity, such as driving a vehicle. It is especially good to practice to the rhythm of your feet when walking, and as you prepare for sleep. This unification with the Divine through your prana and intention is immensely healing.

CONTEMPLATION

Please practice these breathing techniques and note what happens within your body, mind, and emotions and your connection to that which is sacred.

What signals or sensations remind you to practice conscious breathing throughout the day?

Take some time to contemplate your experience with this breathing practice. What shifts occur in your sense of your body/yourself?

CHAPTER 17

TAMING YOUR WAYWARD MIND

Because our daily lives are often hectic, our mind frequently runs away from us and with us. Then we wonder how we moved into strange thoughts and behaviors that have nothing to do with our will or intention. We are often surprised at how our obsessive thoughts take over parts of our lives and leave us wondering who we are, and why our minds seem to have minds of their own, despite our best intentions.

If left unchallenged and uncared for, we can end up with psychological disorders such as anxiety and depression based upon faulty thinking. So, it is of particular importance that we learn to channel our mind's power into grooves that work for us rather than against us. When we can do so, we create new neural pathways in our brain. Our mind then becomes our best friend and works for us in intelligent, productive, and creative ways.

The spiritual practices of meditation, mantra repetition, and prayer are three yogic ways to help our runaway mind relax and open to spiritual dimensions so that it does not have to work so hard and so unproductively.

Over time, with consistent practice, our mind will work in harmony with all of who we are. Then an integration of body, mind, emotion, and spirit that was previously unavailable falls into place. We then find that the clearer and quieter our mind is, the more productive and creative we will be.

This is yoga—a vital and healing union between mind and spirit bringing us to a sacred center within. This yoga opens us to the awareness that we are spiritual beings, that we are connected and guided by something greater than our wayward mind, and that, in this union, we have unlimited powers to create soulful and fulfilling lives.

Any one of the practices of meditation, mantra, and prayer can take us across. All are related and all are highly beneficial. Each of these practices is vital as they each induce quietness and stillness that allows our whole being to soften, open, and connect with All That Is. When our whole being relaxes, we realize that we are not the doers creating heavy, or even mild, pressure upon ourselves. Now we can truly form a spiritual communication and communion with That Which Is Within and That Which Is Without. Now we can come home to our true selves.

Let us begin with the yoga of mantra.

REPEAT YOUR MANTRA

Mantras are bridges between our ordinary thinking and our thought-free state, no matter what is happening in the world around us. As we repeat a mantra, focusing only on the ancient Sanskrit syllables, our mind becomes clear and still. Eventually, the mantra merges into the most beautiful and pure realms of the Divine. Mantra repetition leads us into meditation. It tames our minds by releasing our thoughts rather than being led by them. And mantra repetition is so much more. The Sanskrit syllables themselves are considered sacred. Untold numbers of yoginis and yogis have breathed and chanted them for thousands of years. They are alive with the energies of all ascended masters in the ancient and current lineages. They are a unifying, sanctifying, and powerful yet subtle form of Divine Consciousness, sacred in and of themselves. Repetition of the mantra over and over eventually transforms us into our true Selves, into the pure light of the Divine.

Mantras change our state. They still our mind, give us the ability to focus our thoughts and open us to our higher potentials. At the very least, we become calmer and more connected.

As *Everyday Soul Dancers*, we will practice the ancient and universal mantra HAMSA. (The pronunciation for these syllables is haam saa). This is a mantra, a sound, breathed by all living creatures. These sounds naturally arise and ebb with the inhalation and exhalation of all living beings. When we listen carefully to our breath going in and out, we can hear these syllables. Breathe in with the syllable HAM and exhale with the syllable SA. It is that simple.

All it takes is remembering and then practicing over and over and over. This is a practice to use whenever you remember and, as you practice, you will remember more often.

The translation of HAMSA from Sanskrit into English is I Am That. This mantra signifies and deepens our understanding that I Am a part of All That Is, that the Divine resides within me and that I live and play within the cosmic fields of Divine Consciousness all the days of my life.

Each time we repeat these syllables, we are reinforcing the truth of our being, beyond the snares of the ego. We are honoring our Divinity, our At Oneness with all creation—the people we meet, the natural world, and the people we pray for in war-torn and poverty-stricken countries. As we remember to be At One with everything and everyone, we naturally expand into our greater Selves, we open to ease of being in this world and we honor more deeply our interconnectedness with all of creation. As we practice mantra repetition over time, our negative emotions drop away, our compassion deepens, and we exist in more loving states free of judgments.

Mantra repetition also sustains our energetic body. Over time, it aligns the chakras, strengthening the energies of each one and allowing more light to radiate throughout our being. Simple Sanskrit syllables become mystical gems to carry us home to the numinous world within. When we are on the spiritual path, mantras open the door to our inner world, where we can commune with the wonders of the Divine as She resides within. Such a simple vehicle carries us home to our very most hallowed Selves.

Repeat the mantra HAMSA over and over and over on each inhalation and exhalation while simultaneously slowing your breath into a deep rhythm.

Repeat HAMSA no matter what you are doing.

Repeat HAMSA to still your mind when it is hyperactive, obsessive, or confused.

Repeat HAMSA to simplify your life.

Repeat HAMSA when you are doing chores.

Repeat HAMSA when you are walking, swimming, skiing, stirring a pot, or doing any rhythmic activity. Doing repetitive activities with the mantra in place connects us at a deeper level with the rhythms of the earth, the water, the brilliance of a snow-fallen day, or even the life-filled interior of our homes when we are At One with All That Is.

Repeat HAMSA to help with falling asleep.

Repeat HAMSA to soothe an organ of your body that is in distress or dis-ease.

Repeat HAMSA to connect with your Sacred Self and to That Which is Sacred.

After we have practiced mantra repetition for some time, the syllables of the mantra may drop away as we come into meditation and unite within the sacred field of All That Is. This is one of the gifts of mantra repetition.

The other day I was walking along the beautiful and abundant Truckee River as it runs through the city in which I live. I was practicing the HAM SA mantra in rhythm with my steps. These are some of the connections I made:

I AM the smile on a passing woman's face.

Neon pink and gray hair. I AM she? I question and smile. I AM. I am she. She is my sister, and her friends are my brothers. Inwardly I bow in Namaste to each of them. HAMSA

I AM the energy of the happy connection between her and her friends. HAMSA

I AM the magnificence of the mountains - golden and violet and majestic in the distance at sunset. HAMSA

I AM the flowing river – surging and abundant. HAMSA

I AM the beauty of the earth in all its forms. HAMSA

I AM the lone, snowy-white egret – stately and still and quiet, on a rock in the middle of the river – alone. HAMSA

I AM the flock of ducks – noisy and busy - -convening on the steps above the river, where they hang out even in the middle of a flood. HAMSA

I AM this walk. HAMSA
I AM connected to All That Is. HAMSA
I AM She who flows through me within and without. HAMSA

I AM at peace. HAMSA
I AM quiet. HAMSA
I AM still. HAMSA
I AM. HAMSA.

These words are examples of how the mantra can still our busy mind and join our consciousness to the natural world. As we deepen into this practice, there is so much more to the story. As I practice these syllables and embrace the mystical truths, I know that the Divine, the Sacred, the Mother, the Holy resides within. It is in every feeling I have. It fuels my dream life. It teaches me about love and shows me the ways to stay in alignment with Her. Then when I shift focus outside of myself, I see Her in everything— the rocks, the vibrant colors of autumn, and the shining moon at night.

Later, my feelings change. I am deeply saddened by the marginalization and divisions, the violence and senseless deaths that are so pervasive in far too many places today. We may have many diverse reactions to the daily news stories of lost children, families separated at a border, and people trying to survive and eke out a living in relentlessly war-torn regions. We learn of leaders without moral and historical values who seem to be without regard for others, and, instead, make decisions based upon what is most lucrative for them and their kind. All such stories can cause us to be anxious, fearful, despairing, and helpless; however, on a spiritual path, we learn to focus on those things we can change and to stay prayerful and centered within our lives, even though such travesties and sorrows exist in our world.

Within the realm of lifetimes, we all have been the victims, the perpetrators, and the saviors. In one lifetime or another, we have all been the inquisitors, the artists whose works were destroyed, the witches impaled and burned at the stake, and the ones who watch in horror and do nothing. We also have had experiences of being the priests, the teachers, the wise ones. Within the broad and ancient expanse of our lifetimes, we have experienced it all. These experiences allow us to identify with all the people of our world once our hearts open, and we can see with compassionate eyes, the eyes of love. Repeating the HAMSA mantra, I Am That allows us to identify with those we hear about, both the people suffering and those in power who cause violence and chaos. As we practice these ways, we find that we do not succumb to these damaging emotional states within our own lives. Such a practice goes like this:

I AM the starving children in war-torn countries and far too many communities throughout our world. HAMSA

I AM the mothers and fathers who hold their children without hope. HAMSA

I AM the worldwide government agencies sending aid even though it is not enough. HAMSA

I AM the corrupt leader of any country who allows food supplies to be stolen and out of reach for the people who need them. HAMSA

I AM the person wielding the weapons. HAMSA

I AM the aid worker in a field hospital who cares for the mother, the child, and the soldiers on either side of the conflict. HAMSA

Such a litany can continue throughout our days. It may be disturbing. It also is centering and all-embracing, just like the Divine Feminine. As a result of such a practice, we may look inward and find places in which *we* are conflicted. We may be treating others in lesser ways, or we may be treating ourselves in ways that are demeaning and abusive. All this is worthy of contemplation so that we may release these lesser ways and embrace more soulful ones.

We may decide to act. Perhaps we will make a long, overdue call to a therapist. Perhaps we will donate to a rescue organization.

Perhaps we will find our voice and write to influential government officials. Always we will send prayers for peaceful ways within and without.

One of the effects of the HAMSA practice is that we have an all-embracing view of who we *all* are. Then we become gentler, caring, and loving in our families and communities. At the very least, the HAMSA mantra reminds us of our humanity throughout our lifetimes. It helps us release judgments of others, and to pray for them instead. These repetitions, over time, can open us to positive actions and soulful living. HAMSA is a centering practice that brings us both expanded vision and equanimity in the face of it all. With such equanimity, our intentions are clearer, and our ways of living more skillful and soulful. The overarching energies of the Mother see it all. We can learn to do likewise. And then it is our actions, prayers, and centering ways that make a difference in Her world which is our world.

She is everywhere! This is an amazing piece of good news. My consciousness expands into the furthest reaches of the cosmos, and into the tiny smallness of that trail of sugar ants making their way into my home. Then I see Her and know Her in every one of us despite the personas and costumes we wear each day. I know Her in the miracle of a newborn, and in the family's grief at a loved one's death. Our tears become Her tears that flow and our anger fires within Her fire for justice and equality. Her darkness impels us to thrive and to search for the light. It is Her joy that we dance and Her songs that we sing. Her ecstasy is ever-present in our creativity, our sensuality, and our passion. She calls us to express all the myriad parts of who She is. Her very essence flows through these simple Sanskrit syllables and the silence in between each one as She mirrors Herself back to us in all our acts.

Practice this mantra over and over and over to return home to your most sacred Self. Eventually you will find that HAMSA continues within you without any thought.

Elaine Hoem

CONTEMPLATION

Practice HAMSA to be in communion with other people, with other living beings, with the beauty of the earth, and with inanimate objects.

Write about your experience repeating this mantra.

What are the ways you can strengthen this practice?

CHAPTER 18

MEDITATION

Meditation is a foundational spiritual practice that moves us from the distracting and obsessive thoughts of the mind to a pure and quiet place within, into a space that is open and clear. Any time we go beyond our active minds, wondrous experiences can take place. When we attain that serene, pure space, we begin to experience That Which is Sacred. It is always a gift when this happens because then we know, without a doubt, that we are a part of the purity and Oneness of All That Is, that this purity is inside of us, and it is who we are. In these moments, we know that we reside in Her heart, that we are enveloped by Her energies and Her grace, and that She also dwells within *us*. This is an awe-inspired knowing that changes our perspective about everything. It reduces our belief in our unworthiness. It opens us to universal consciousness energies so that healing can take place. During meditation, we open to greater wisdom. Our emotions calm. Our creativity may surprise us. When we awaken to our loving nature, we change the state of our body/ mind and expand the possibilities of our lives.

During times of meditation, we become free of ego. Our boundaries and sense of doer-ship in trying to control our lives no longer hold sway. Instead, these vagaries of the mind begin to dissolve, and we meld into the sacred state of who we are. We open to the truth of HAMSA. I am at One with my God/Goddess Self. There is no separation. I Am. I Am That. I am larger and greater than my mind.

As we continue to meditate over time, this knowledge stays with us throughout our waking and sleep states. Our minds become clearer, and we greatly reduce negative thoughts. We become peaceful no matter what is happening around us. Different emotional upsets vanish, and, at times, physical ailments may disappear. Our ordinary daily tasks become full of ease and soul filled. Doing so creates different ways of being, which, in turn, change our karma in this life and our destiny in this life and the next ones.

As we deepen our knowledge of our inner Self, we begin to live more and more from the center of our sacred worthiness. Then our outer, daily lives noticeably change. Our ways of living in the world become reflective of our inner state. We live in peace and openness, and we more easily love and care for others and ourselves. Increasingly, we become clearer about the best ways to be in any situation.

As beautiful as this state of being is, we must also remember that we are human and, therefore, not perfect meditating machines. Because of this, we can be thrown off-center for short or longer periods. This is normal and a part of our human and spiritual experience. However, once we remember that we are beginning what will be a lifetime practice, it becomes easier to return to meditation and to enter once again into this state of grace.

While there are many ways to meditate, the practice I recommend is to commit to sitting for meditation daily. This is a practice in Constancy. It is usually wise to begin the practice by sitting for 10 minutes, gradually increasing the minutes over time. An erect posture is important so that the universal life energies, or the Kundalini Shakti, can move freely within. Having a focal point is important when learning this practice. Focusing on our breathing in slow and measured ways helps to shift our attention from our thoughts to a focus only on the breath. Later, some practices add a mantra to further movement toward Divine Consciousness and to our inner awareness.

Once you decide to meditate, there are ways to hold a yogic posture that will add to your experience. First, allow your spine to elongate from the base of your spine to the crown of your head. Draw your shoulders back and down and tilt your jaw slightly back towards your neck. If you like, sit on a chair that supports your back with your feet parallel and on the floor with your legs in a comfortable position. Feel free to use cushions to be comfortable. Relax and breathe deeply into and out of your belly.

If you sit on the floor, sitting on a meditation cushion raises your hips above your knees. If you sit in a cross-legged position, it is fine to support your knees with cushions. In any position, fold your hands, resting one over the other in your lap, or you can place your hands on your knees with your thumbs and forefingers touching.

If you are more comfortable lying down, find a posture that is easy on your back. Supporting your legs at the knees with cushions takes the strain off your spine.

Now, focus naturally on your breath, allowing it to move freely, slowly, and deeply. There is no strain, only ease. Some people close their eyes; some simply lower their gaze and soften it. When you are relaxed, inhale HAM and exhale SA over and over. If thoughts come to your mind, allow them to float through as if they are clouds slowly moving away. Then return to the mantra. Meditation requires relaxation and a subtle focus on the inner world rather than the outer one. Please be very gentle with yourself as you ease into these soulful ways. They take time and practice. There is no right or wrong; there is simply a return to an awareness of where you are in this moment.

Stay with this practice as long as you are comfortable. Initially, this could be a few minutes. Over time, you will want to sit for longer periods.

At the end of every meditation, it is important to become aware of your body and its position on the chair, floor, or cushions. Focus again on your breath, breathing deeply and slowly. Feel grounded on the earth again. Then gently open your eyes or raise your gaze and absorb all that is around you. Please walk for a time to ground yourself and especially before driving. Also, drink plenty of water to hydrate and to help with the release of toxins. Take care to preserve the quiet state you have attained for as long as possible. If you lose this quiet awareness, please take note of what took you away from it and then let that thought go as well. Breathe.... Then return to your quiet state once again.

Many things may happen in meditation, particularly as we begin to practice regularly. One of the first shifts that we notice is that we have is that we become still, and we find that our minds are at peace. As we continue to turn within, we feel the energy of universal consciousness or the Goddess Kundalini Shakti flowing through us. Sometimes Her ways are most subtle, with energy flowing lightly throughout our bodies. Sometimes Her ways are fierce, astonishing, and unlike anything we have experienced before. At times, we reside in a velvety black void.

Some people see visions, lights, or colors. Some see angels or other ascended beings. Over time, other startling, complex, and amazing visions may come to you. You may find that there is energy activated within, running up and down your spine or centered in different parts in your body. In this way, our lives change. After the meditation, we may find that our world looks different, more alive, and with brighter colors. We may feel softer, and more open while attaining a sense of calmness and awe. Sometimes these energies take the form of mudras, sacred hand positions that stabilize the spiritual energy in our body. Whatever happens is the work of the Goddess Kundalini Shakti, who is moving within to clear out old and toxic energies, and to turn *you* into a golden vessel of loving grace.

Because we are opening our awareness to Spirit, some of us may receive messages that have to do with issues that we are dealing with in our lives. For others, it may seem that nothing is happening. All these experiences are to be honored. They are gifts and worthy of contemplation and action, if appropriate; however, they are not the end of this journey. The journey of meditation takes us to a place where we are in communion with That Which Is Sacred within, a place where we can then allow these energies to flow through us and out into our world.

All these states are customary meditative experiences. When you return to your waking consciousness, take some time to reflect on your experiences, to contemplate and write about them. Doing so will help you grow in untold ways. For the most part, there is nothing to fear; however, if you have questions or concerns, it is vital to share them with an experienced meditation teacher.

During those times in which it seems that nothing is happening and that you seem to be struggling with your mind, do not give up. Patience with the process is required. Keep sitting for meditation daily. Each time you do, you might want to offer a prayer and set an intention for a more viable connection to That Which Is Sacred. Keep going forward with this practice, day by day. Eventually, these resistances will dissipate, and you will move more deeply into the state of meditation with greater ease, finding it possible to meditate even while waiting in a doctor's office, standing in line at a store, or just before falling asleep.

The only times we must not meditate are while driving, operating machinery, or doing an activity that needs our full attention.

Otherwise, wherever we are, we can return to the breath and the mantra. HAMSA...HAMSA.... Even if we do this for only a few minutes, we are honoring ourselves as spiritual beings, quieting our minds, and uplifting the energies within us and around us.

Always honor yourself for sitting to meditate. Do not judge your meditations or compare your experiences with others; rather, be curious and attentive to each meditative experience. New neural pathways are forming. These pathways strengthen the connections with those parts of us that open to sacred experiences within. Honor even the meditations that seem difficult knowing that you have committed to this practice, that you are focusing your mind on the present, and that you are in training as a spiritual being. This is sufficient and wonderful, as the sacred energies are doing their inimitable dances—a clearing here, a sadness there, anger being expelled, a solution to a gnarly problem, a softening, a falling into grace, a deepening, and an expansion. Sometimes you may experience visions of other realms and ascended beings showing you the way. In meditation, gifts are given, karma is cleared, and addictive habits can drop away. Addictions and lesser ways of being become much less important in our lives as our spiritual communion becomes more constant and vital.

Often it is helpful to meditate with others, and today, there are smartphone and computer apps to use whenever you want to practice and need further instruction and imagery. Search out these aids. Eventually, you may be led to a spiritual teacher who can lead you further into your inner sacred states. At the end of nine chapters, you will find links to recorded meditations you can access on my website: www.everydaysouldances.com/meditations. I have included these meditations to get you started if you are new to this practice. And, if you already meditate, you might want to use these meditations to foster different experiences.

When we meditate, we may not be able to see obvious changes, yet over time, we are somehow more than we were at the beginning.

Even when we feel that nothing is happening, the practice of sitting for meditation *is* meditation. Eventually, you will notice changes within and without.

The practices of mantra repetition, contemplation, prayer, conscious breathing, and setting intentions are all wonderful preparatory exercises that both strengthen and soften your mind to open doorways to your eternal Self. Meditating with an experienced meditation teacher and a group of like-minded meditators also opens energetic gateways to enter into this Divine state. Listening to guided imagery leading into meditation also prepares one's mind to enter such states. Please listen to the meditations as often as you would like. They will add focus to your practice.

LAKE MEDITATIONS

YOU AND THE LAKE AND ONENESS

Follow the link below or scan the QR code with your smartphone to access this meditation through the website: www.everydaysouldances.com/meditations.

SUNSET MEDITATION

You will find the recording of this meditation through the QR code below. It links you to www.everydaysouldances.com/meditations.

Elaine Hoem

CONTEMPLATION

Write about your experiences of meditation.

Write about any new images, insights, and awarenesses that have come to you in meditation.

If you need to strengthen your commitment to meditate, how will you do this and what inner and outer resources will you access?

CHAPTER 19

YOUR GOLDEN HEART

We all know that our physical heart is a most astounding organ, doing its work from our first to our last breath. We are aware of its beat and the gift of our life force with each beat. In our society, there is great information about the care of our physical hearts—what to eat, how much to exercise, the risks of being sedentary, the medicines to take, and the amazing surgeries to keep our hearts and our lives in place after "cardiac events." Our technologies and medicines have given many of us the gift of much longer and healthier lives than previous generations had. We are fortunate indeed, and our lives take on greater purpose because we have greater vitality, life force, and longevity. So now, the questions become "How will I live this amazing life that has been granted to me?" and "What is my destiny?"

These questions lead us to explore the heart chakra, which is an equally astonishing energy center that holds our spiritual essence. It has been called the *Seat of the Soul.* Our hearts hold our wonder, our joy, our astonishment, and our infinite capacity to love. This energetic heart also is one of the repositories of our wounding, our brokenness, and the pain we deal with during this life and past lifetimes. It is often within this heart center that we feel our grief, our isolation, our fears, and our deep sadness. When the heart chakra opens during the spiritual journey, we awaken to our true Selves and to the divinity that resides within us. This is no small thing. In fact, with this opening, previous wounding and negative karmas release and many other spiritual gifts are given. When this happens, we step into a lightness of being, which is our true home.

When we are ego-bound, our hearts may seem closed, broken, defended, and holding a lot of pain from past and present experiences. During these times, we might close others out, and we fear deep connection and intimacy. Our defenses can be mighty fortresses that seem impenetrable. A defended heart comes from the experiences in our past and present lives in which we were traumatized, rejected, scared, or violated. These defenses continue to remain in place until we become spiritually ready to open to All That Is and to allow these defenses to fall away through psychological work and our spiritual practices.

Logically we cannot know what will cause the heart to open. However, if it is our dharma to open to our spiritual essence in a particular lifetime, this will happen in one way or another. This we can count on. This is a vital part of our destiny of a particular lifetime. We can foster such openings by becoming conscious and searching for our higher meaning and our higher Self.

When our hearts open, we receive newer and greater awareness and the ability to drop our judgments, our black and white thinking, and our view of other people as faulty and something to be feared. When this happens, karmic blockages to our ability to understand the ways of our soul fall away, and our communion with the Divine becomes brilliant and clear. Then everything changes within our energetic being. Our outer relationships become lighter, more loving, and free. When our defenses drop away, we may find answers to problems we are having, and it becomes clearer as to how to live in our newly awakened lives.

As our heart opens further, our vision expands beyond ordinary seeing because we are connecting our vision to our heart, this brilliant spiritual center that is at the hub of our being. Now we more easily forgive what needs to be forgiven and open to much deeper and more expanded acts of loving—loving our lives and our sacred natures, all our relations, our earth, and yes, even our enemies. At this point, we may experience joy, trust, and amazement even in the most ordinary of things—the scent of a rose, the brilliance of a bird's feathers and songs, the stunning beauty of the moonrise. The opening of the heart sets a new stage upon which we live our lives. It shows us ways to live our unique and highest dharma. We also become clearer as to how our dharma interweaves itself with that of all others.

One of the concepts we learn along the way in working with energy is that the spiritual, the karmic, and the emotional can all inform and change conditions of the physical body. For example, if we have fears about illness, these fears can eventually create the disease itself or a worsening of a physical condition. Therefore, we must always pay attention to the conditions of both our physical and our energetic hearts—clearing what needs to be healed at the spiritual, emotional, and psychological levels to protect and strengthen the physical heart and to open to our more expanded, loving energetic hearts. This is where the work of skillful psychotherapists and wise healers can be of great assistance as they can see within and beyond what we can see on our own.

Broken Heart Syndrome is a cardiac problem that has fascinated me since I first read about it. The medical names for this syndrome are "Stress Cardiomyopathy," "Takotsubo Cardiomyopathy," or "Apical Ballooning Syndrome." The symptoms are like those of a heart attack. This cardiac event usually happens in women and after a sudden, traumatic loss.[9] The medical treatment is the same as treatment for a heart attack; however, an echocardiogram will reveal that there are no blockages in the arteries thus no heart attack. The ECG reveals that the left ventricle of the heart is barely functioning and not pumping blood in a normal fashion. Once the acute stress has subsided, a follow-up ECG reveals normal heart functioning once again. Preventative measures have to do with managing stress, breathing exercises, and overall heart-healthy recommendations regarding exercise and good nutrition.

There is no separation between our physical heart, our emotional heart, and our spiritual heart. While we can treat a physical heart problem with good cardiac care or a problem of loss or grief with good psychotherapy, we are one glorious whole. Anything we do to achieve better physical/emotional/ spiritual health will affect all parts of our being. Realizing this always brings me to a state of awe and a recommitment to good care at all levels of my being.

There may be many layers of karmic constrictions overlaying our hearts from former wounding in this lifetime and past ones. As we engage in our spiritual practices, one layer after another falls away. Sometimes this is obvious in large ways, such as the cracking open of the energetic heart. This experience can happen during intense meditation. At other times, the openings are more subtle. All of them will become more evident over time, however, when we realize that we are treating ourselves or others differently and with more love. An open heart naturally brings us into more loving relationships. Boundaries and judgments fall away. The glowing beauty of a golden, open heart radiates light, bringing about a deepening union that affects everything in our world.

If an open heart can accomplish all of this, and we are able to open it with conscious intention, then why do we not live our lives this way all the time? Another dance that we seem to engage in often is one of protecting our wounded hearts from others and from situations that dishonor and cause pain. On the other hand, as spiritual beings, we want our hearts to be open to others and to all of life that is available to us. This interplay can be tricky as we practice being as open as possible to all that life is presenting to us and to learn to view obstacles, difficult medical conditions, and seemingly difficult people as opportunities for spiritual growth. Along the way, we will also learn when it is appropriate to set boundaries in problematic situations to protect our delicate hearts.

As we practice staying open, our suffering diminishes, and we heal what needs healing. When we close our hearts, our tiny selves do their untrained dances that can harm, diminish, disconnect, and degrade. When we retreat, we will likely stay stuck and unhappy, living a less informed and conscious life. As we honor the challenges that have to do with both protecting and opening our beautiful hearts, we learn to always move forward with appropriate boundaries in place and a willingness to open into states of forgiveness.

When we practice these dances, we honor each act in which we can open our hearts to what is happening in the now. We release ways of being that no longer serve. An open heart, a loving act, and a deep honoring of others and ourselves are all beautiful and poignant heart gifts that will build upon themselves. These are the gifts of flowing freedom, enhanced joy of living, deeper intimacy, deep peace, and states of being that were previously unimagined.

The spiritual teachers speak of how our lives change when we bring an open and aware heart to all our life's tasks. This is what we learn and live while on a spiritual path. When these shifts occur, our ways transform, our intentions clear, and our acts become strong and gentle. Living in such gentle ways, we infuse even simple tasks with the energies of love as we continually open to our spiritual essence. Each time we remember to breathe and bring Prana to our sacred heart space, we fill ourselves with wonder and light. Healing at all levels of our being can and does, happen, especially when we release old karma and heal our brokenness. Then our heart's home is a golden and rightful place to honor the Goddess and to create a heart temple for Her so that we remember that She resides within us always.

A friend shared this story about his closed and then opened heart. You can see how dramatically his life changed after a spiritual experience in which his heart "cracked open." We also learn how personal trauma can wound the fiber of our relationships and how both therapy and spiritual experiences help to weave us into a new wholeness.

My friend is longing for something beyond the neglect and trauma of his earlier life. He spent most of his life in depressive states of lesser and greater severity. He and his partner are disconnected. His coolness towards her has led to a detachment from her. At the same time, she wants more communication and intimacy. Their relationship is dull, utilitarian, and in trouble.

He wants to make a change. He begins a search for how to live beyond the constraints that his life has held for him up to this point. His first step is to participate in therapy. In therapy, he can talk about some of his early childhood and young adult traumatic experiences. These experiences had remained hidden deep within. After finding his voice and speaking about these experiences, he is surprised to discover that, in the naming of his suffering, and having it witnessed, he has become free of some of his anguish for the first time.

After this change of thinking, he decides to go on a meditation retreat even though he is not completely open and more than a little skeptical. While there, despite himself and his defenses, he has a strong spiritual awakening. His closed heart breaks open with a huge internal cracking sound. Uncontrollable sobbing follows. His tears stun him, as he has never been a person who cried. At this moment, his defenses drop away.

When he returns from the retreat, he notices that his need for isolation lessens, and his desire for love begins to awaken and becomes crystal clear. He knows that this experience was a much-needed spiritual transformation and a miracle of the highest order.

As time passes after this experience, he becomes more open to his partner. The couple enters couples therapy and learns, for the first time, positive communication skills and new ways to bring harmony, soulfulness, and excitement into their relationship.

HEALING YOUR GOLDEN HEART MEDITATION

This meditation encourages you to release old heart blockages. It then draws you into your heart's essence, to its beauty and radiant potential.

Please listen to the recorded meditation by following the QR code below to www:everydaysouldances.com/meditations.

CONTEMPLATION

Write about your physical heart and your energetic heart,

Its wounding

Its protection

Its openness and its capacity for love.

Write about your experience with this heart meditation.

CHAPTER 20

THE YOGA OF PRAYER

It is nighttime. My sister and I are on our knees by our beds.
My mother is watching over us and guiding us.

Now I lay me down to sleep.
I pray the Lord my soul to keep.
If I should die before I wake,
I pray the Lord my soul to take.
Amen. [10]

In childhood and early adulthood, I loved the Gregorian chants and the incense and rituals of the Catholic Church. I called upon the Blessed Mother long ago. She provided comfort to me as a child and a teen when life seemed broken and I did not understand what was happening. Through these rituals, the music, and my prayers, She was there for me. I could count on Her for solace.

Hail Mary, full of grace.
The Lord is with Thee.
Blessed is the fruit of Thy womb, Jesus.
Holy Mary,
Mother of God,
Pray for us
Now and at the hour of our death.
Amen

Today I bow down to the Mother and my teachers.
My simple prayer is:

Open me. Heal me. Show me the way.
May I be fully surrendered to Your grace-filled ways.

May Your ways, Your words, Your wisdom always move through me.
May all people be healed.
May all of us open to our highest potentials.
May I know only love. May I love many and may I love deeply.
Namaste

One day several years ago, She spoke to me. These are Her words:

I am the beauty of the lake,
The strength of the mountains, the change of seasons,
The spaciousness of the sky.
I am in wind whispers, in storms,
And in the voices of birds singing my glory.
I am the colorful quiet of the sunrise
And the brilliant peace of the setting sun.

I am of the realm of all that is holy
And all that is wise.
I am the truth.

My magnificence and beneficence arise
From the depths of my being
From the center of the universe.
It is fire from this center that brings you power
And it is from my heavens that you become light.

My soul and spirit are found in all acts of creation,
In messages received from the beauties of the earth
And in truths spoken by your sisters and brothers
In their loving and their struggles.

I AM so that you can be.
Know that you know Me and that you reside in Me
And I in you.
Know that we are One.

I am the Lady of the Lake.
Some call Me God.
And you are the people of the Lake.
You are My Divinity in human form.

It is you who have My ancientness coursing through your veins,
And you who see My glories and give them names.
It is you who searches beneath the surface of the mind
Through pain and healing
For hidden treasures I offer
To bring My truths to light.

You are co-creators with Me.
Open your heart and you shall know Me
For I reside in you in the form of love
In the palace of your heart.

I am in you in joy, and mystery,
And in the gentle loving greatness
That is your search, your transformation, and your life.

Remember Me.
And remember who you are
In My truth, beauty, and love.

I AM
YOU ARE
WE ARE ONE
HAMSA

These words are the words of our Mother. Her imagery shows us our vast interconnections with Her, with one another, with All That Is. Within Her scintillating, infinite, and all-embracing cosmic arms, we are all related. We are all, every one of us, brothers and sisters to each other. We also are intimately related to Her, to all the saints, angels, and other ascended masters. We are all a part of one teeming cosmic field of Divine Consciousness. There is no separation, no discrimination.

145

Her arms carry only love. Our task always is to find ways to enter such far-reaching love, with each other, and with the pantheon of all these lighted beings here to guide us to our true home. The spiritual path encourages us to release all blockages in the way of such love, and then to surrender to it. As we grow in our supreme worthiness, these artificial concepts drop away, and we see all of us worthy in the light of Divine Consciousness. We are not only all related; we are interrelated, each influencing others with our thoughts, prayers, actions, and deeds. This ultimate union is yoga.

Another way to say this in today's terms is that every one of us is playing in a quantum field made of energy and vibration. Knowing that each of our acts has consequences throughout this vast cosmic field changes our state. We become more careful, more loving, and more empathetic to those who do not yet know these ways. The knowing of these immense connections leads us home, to peaceful living, to soulful living, and heartfelt prayers for our world and ourselves.

In my prayers and meditations, I often see the truth of these words. We each are woven into this amazing energetic, luminous, vibrating, and ever-changing tapestry that is the web of life. Prayer provides the threads within this vast tapestry to weave together all communions with each other and with the Divine. When we pray, our thoughts resound within and throughout this teeming web of life. What we do to and for one another, the good, the brilliant, the bad, and the ugly reverberates within the souls of all. It is through the yoga of prayer that we clarify our intentions and our thoughts. We release and heal emotional distress, our emotions are cleansed, and our ways lightened.

Prayer is a bridge, a communication, and a communion that connects us to all others and to the Mother, the angels, and ascended masters. It is a way to access our inimitable and vast spirit. It carries us beyond our sense of smallness into the wonders of our sacred ways. It is a way for our deepest needs and highest intentions to be heard, and for transformations to be set in motion. These changes happen first at the energetic level and then, with our directed intention and attention, proceed to create changes in the emotional and physical levels.

This is the yoga of prayer—the essence of our union with All That Is and with one another. We are all a part of a vast, yet intimate, energetic, cosmic, and sacred surprise that moves through us, within us and without, always. When we pray, we know that there is more to the story than our ego-based thinking, than our tiny selves. We become humble when we open our hearts and ask for help. In our humility, our prayers are heard. We can count on this being so.

Through prayer, we do our part to set energies in motion that will create positive change for ourselves, for others, and our world. Since we are all a part of one Divine Consciousness, the energies of prayer are far-reaching. We can count on them having a positive impact on the people and situations we hold in our prayers. Our energies are alive! They are imbued with those scintillating energies of our Mother, and they are enhanced by all that She is, by Her grace, and by Her energy living within us.

When we open to Her energetic pathways, we have access to Her wisdom, to our greatest healing potential, and infinitely transformative states of being. We are active participants on a cosmic stage, and all other beings are there as well, available to assist us when we ask for help. Once we understand this, the only disruptions to these connections are those we create by staying in our ego-based selves or by having illusions that we are in control, or by simply forgetting that these sacred connections exist. While the great Ones are always available to us, we are not always available to Them and to what is possible in communion with Them.

In prayer, we surrender those parts of ourselves that need to be in control and mistakenly believe that we have all the answers. Instead, we listen and discover that the answers to our prayers come from many places and take many forms. At times, the words we hear within, or without, are unmistakably clear and direct guidance from the Mother. At other times, the answer comes unexpectedly from a friend or acquaintance who tells a story or says the perfect words to guide us farther on our path.

When we open our eyes and listen closely, Nature, one of the faces of the Goddess, gives answers easily. The water has lessons to teach about fluidity and flow. The mountains show us majesty, strength, grounding, and stability. The stars are always our guides into the mysteries of what life is about in its most expansive form. The moon and her tides awaken the rhythms within us that call us home. The sun always reminds us of our own inner and outer golden light.

When we look and listen with open awareness and wonder, we find that She is always speaking to us. She is everywhere—within and without, in our sorrows and grief, in our joys and ecstasies, in our complete lack of comprehension and confusion, and our moments of total understanding of our state of oneness with Her. She is in all the myriad forms of loving—in the heartbreaks and the heart mends. All forms of healing come from Her. And when our prayers are answered and we have been touched by Her grace, we bow deeply to our inner Self, and, in those moments, we are made whole.

We pray for help and for guidance, to know the ways that are clear and of the highest order. The answers to our prayers show the way. Then our actions give grounding to our prayers. In this way, our lives change. We inextricably connect to our divinity—a communion that is always present any and every time we ask. Our forgetfulness can call us away from this communion; our remembering brings us home in an instant.

As we lay bare our souls in prayer, over time, we begin to sense that we have entered states of grace within the realm of the mystic. We experience a deepening of our intuitiveness. From that space, we become consciously aware of the falsehood of our ego-driven self's belief that we are alone. In its place, we find that we are co-creators with the Divine Feminine and other ascended beings who are there to sustain us. We are never alone, and we have no limitations.

Now we see that our responsibility is to stay open to our guidance, knowing that it can manifest in so many forms. We might hear a direct message from the Mother, or the message we need may come from something we have read or heard another say. It may come from a change in our state—a softening, a shift in energy, a dream message—that we learn to follow. We co-create by watching, listening, and being open. To do so, we focus our attention on receiving the answers as we remember the content of our original prayer—our question or our request or one made on behalf of someone or something else. I am always humbled and grateful when such messages come to me. Each time I follow them they are always right and may have huge ramifications for me, for my work, or for others. I increasingly heard such messages when I was writing this book—direct ones that sometimes came at unusual times. I made sure to write them down. Later they became strong and essential words for this book.

Prayer is our calling out to the energies of that which is Sacred. It takes us beyond the ordinary and makes our ordinary ways sacred. When we remember to pray, we bring the energies of the Divine Feminine into our actions. Then all our ways become lighted, more peaceful, and more loving no matter what is happening in our external world. When we pray, we soften, relax, and become more open and trusting. As we open in prayer, we open our hearts, our vision expands, and we experience our Oneness with All That Is.

There are so very many forms of prayer. A simple and effective prayer that we can use at any time is to ask: *What is the highest that I am meant to accomplish today? Please show me the way.*

The following prayers are those that have poignancy for me as a Soul Dancer. They are all-encompassing. Consider the ones most compelling for you and then enter prayerful states with them.

INTENTION INTO MANIFESTATION

In this prayer, we set an intention for what is important to us. Then we imagine dropping this intention into our heart, imbuing it with lighted heart energies and the beauty and perfection of our heart center. Next, we visualize the outcome we want with as much energy, specificity, and vitality as we can imagine. We create the desired outcome in our mind first, imagining that it already has come to fruition in expansive, rich, and beautiful ways beyond our original imagining. Holding this image, we then pray to the Mother with this simple request:

If this desire is of the highest for my soul's growth and the highest good of others, please give Your blessings so that it can become manifest.

If your request is for another, pray:

If this desire is of the highest for _____*'s soul's growth, please give Your blessings so that will manifest.*

After setting an intention, we can let this visualization and prayer go. We might want to revisit it occasionally, but we do not need to. The energies for our intentions have been set in motion and they will shift and change of their own accord for the highest good. We can trust that our prayer has been received. Now our role is to trust that the highest energies have been set in motion.

PRAYER TO SHIFT PERCEPTIONS AND PERSPECTIVES

Sometimes we pray for a particular situation in our lives. We pray for wisdom, insight, and ways to move forward. When we know that we are confused in our perspective due to the ways of our ego, we can pray that our perception changes to a more soulful one. It often is amazing to me to see the rapid shifts that can take place in my thoughts. While we may ask for specific solutions to problems, we may not know what is best for us, for the other, or what karmic conditions are being played out. We may state that we are open to what is highest and best for us beyond what we are currently able to see.

I use this form of prayer when I find myself obsessing about a situation or relationship. Usually, I feel caught in something that I do not know how to handle. This is the ideal situation to pray for a change in perspective. I pray:

I know I am off base and anxious regarding this situation. I cannot see a way out, a better way to be. I know that I am confused. Please help me to shift my perspective to a more enlightened one, to see clearly, to see the truth of this situation. Once I have a clearer insight, I will do what I know to do. Perhaps it will be best to do nothing. I am grateful always.

Namaste

Then I can let these worries go, trusting that I will be granted clear insight. Often this shift in the state of my mind will happen immediately. This is an amazing prayer for holding our minds in a clear and quiet state.

~

FROM THE PERSONAL TO THE UNIVERSAL

Because we know that we are all interconnected, our energies can reach out to a particular person and to all people who are in similar situations. For example, when my family is traveling, I pray that they are safe. Then I ask that all people traveling on this day also have safe journeys. An additional, all-encompassing prayer is one in which I ask that all people everywhere be safe and protected always, and that which is of the highest for all people become manifest. Through such prayers, our world changes as these high and all-inclusive energies reach out to whoever is ready to receive them.

Please read the example below and then practice expanding your prayer to be as inclusive as possible.

Oh, most Compassionate One, please be with my son and his wife and children as they travel. May they be safe wherever they are. May all fellow travelers also be safe and free from harm. May all those they meet along the way be kind, compassionate, and helpful. May the cities of their destinations hold only positive energies. May all people everywhere be safe and free from harm. May all of us grow into the highest, grace-filled versions of ourselves.

May we all be safe and comforted. I thank You for always being with me and for hearing my prayers.

Namaste

Often it is difficult to have compassion when we have angst and deep sorrow regarding those who are violent and those who perpetrate evil in our world. We may not be able to understand such cruelty, thoughtlessness, anger, and violence; however, when we see others as only evil and beyond redemption, we are holding onto dualities of right and wrong and thus limiting possibilities beyond what we can currently see. When we remember that these people are broken or unconscious, we will understand that they may have obvious karma to undo. Perhaps they are acting in such egregious ways to serve a much needed and larger karmic purpose that we are not capable of seeing with ordinary eyes. Our prayer can be one of asking that such people and all people, including ourselves, find those sacred openings that show us the ways to that which is greater than our current state. In such a prayer, we set energies in motion beyond the current situation. As we remember the lessons of karma running throughout lifetimes, we understand more easily that within each of us, all things will right themselves, if not in this lifetime, then in another.

This day I grieve when I see the horrors of families living in the war-torn regions around the world. I feel helpless and hopeless. I do not understand how we humans can be so callous as to hurt each other in such far-reaching and violent ways. I am asking you, the Divine Mother, to magnify these prayer energies with Your grace so that they may reach all who are available to receive them. I ask that the suffering of all men, women, and children lessen due to the right action of those who are available to help. I ask that Your energies open those involved who are ready to make shifts so that they may do so. May they somehow receive those energies that have to do with decreasing violence and increasing capacities for non-violence and benevolence. I ask that the leaders of countries who are involved also awaken. I trust that eventually many of those involved will open their hearts and lay aside their hatred and violence. I ask that the aid organizations do their part so that the right aid reaches all who need it. I ask that all leaders have strong, clear, and compassionate voices. I ask that all countries are

moving closer to non-violent solutions to their divisions. I pray that Your lighted ways reach into the darkest realms to foster all possible changes for the good of all.
  Namaste

Within each prayer, we learn to embrace All That Is as a part of our humanity, our learning in this life, and our expansion into more sacred states. Our story always reveals itself through sacred assistance. And we are learning that we are co-creators with the Divine Feminine and other ascended beings who are there to sustain us along the way. As we pray, we send our heartfelt thoughts on high, and we capture these thoughts deep within so that *we become the prayer*. In these ways, we are strengthened by such sacred intention.

It is right and good to pray for the leaders of our country and all countries so that they can govern fairly for *all* people. We ask that those who know better but remain silent find their voice. Where there is war, we pray for the refugees, for the countries who will accept them, for the aid workers, and for the new communities that will form with new groups of people. We pray that these people be welcomed into their new communities.

Each person and every group of people and their nations all have unique karmas and dharmas to live out. This is all a part of the cosmic dance of our lives and far beyond what we can foresee. When we pray for all, we contribute to energies of potentials, possibilities, and peace throughout our world, and we consciously intend that our world draw closer to wholeness, that all karmas for all people be resolved, and that all of us rise to our highest potentials.

And because we all have shadow sides with which we too have hurt, controlled, or abused others, we ask to make these hidden parts of ourselves obvious so that we can do the necessary work of clearing our specific karmas, forgiving ourselves and others involved, making amends to others, and then living our lives in more enlightened ways. As we do this shadow work, we are much less likely to demonize those who hold the center stage with anger, abuse, and negativity. We pray for every one of us to learn from our experiences, to grow, open and change so that we all move in the direction of the lighted ways of the Sacred.

THE YOGA OF BLESSING ONE
ANOTHER AND OURSELVES

The Mother is always blessing us. We only need open to Her and Her ways to sense Her blessings, often many times a day. It is our dharma to be Her eyes and thoughts so that we are reaching out for Her and sending Her blessings to specific people and situations in our lives.

I love sending blessings to one specific person or a group of people. This form of prayer can be a spontaneous one that we offer anytime we think of someone. This is an effective way to shift our thoughts from obsessing about another or a difficulty in a relationship. Rather than ruminating or worrying, we bless the other person or the situation, ourselves, and all people involved; then we ask that the highest good happens for all involved. Once we do this, it is easier to let go and to clear our minds knowing that we have done the best we know to do at this time.

We can bless the people in the waiting room with us and the drivers on the road. We may bless a homeless person or those out for a bike ride. Any time we obsess over thoughts of another, we can bless that person and ourselves, asking that these lesser energies transform into higher states for each of us.

Before an interview or a meeting that could be stressful, it is good to send a positive intention for the interview or meeting itself, and then to bless all others involved as well as yourself. I like to see the entire situation surrounded by Divine light that casts its rays into the room and gently touches each person involved.

We can give a similar blessing before surgery or any other medical procedure to set an intention of the highest good for the patient and for each medical person involved. In such a blessing, we ask that the Mother and all ascended masters and angels surround everyone and everything with light—the patient and the procedure as well all the medical staff that are assisting. This helps the patient be less anxious and better prepared. The energies of the Goddess and the healing angels become a vital and lighted part of the procedure and the healing afterward.

Such prayers are so simple that one might doubt their effectiveness; however, once we remember that the Goddess resides within each of us and that Her energies are carried far and wide, we will also remember that it is a part of our dharma to bless others. The more we are in a state of blessing, the higher our energies are for ourselves and others. When we are in a state of near-constant prayer, everything changes.

We can always go one step farther so that we are adding to the possibilities and love in the world. We can always be more soulful in our approaches. For example, when someone has a birthday, we can say Happy Birthday in an uninspired voice, or we can say Happy Birthday with enthusiasm and then add heartfelt thoughts that speaks directly to the other's heart. These simple practices reach far into the heart of goodness and soulful ways.

This is my blessing to you:

Dear One,

I have deep gratitude that you have followed along so far with these Soul Dances. I pray for you to receive abundant grace through these words and other lighted ways. May only that which is of the highest come your way. May you be well, healed, and filled with joy. May you be strengthened by love, feel loved, and be love.

May you continue to receive the energies of this blessing through all your days. May all your practices of coming home to the Divine bear fruit in all parts of your life. May you live a life filled with the wonder, transformation, and adventures of the Divine every day.

Namaste

Now please bless yourself.

PRAYERS OF GRATITUDE

At any time of the day, and especially in the evenings before falling asleep, please take a few moments to feel a heartfelt thanksgiving for all you have received during the day. By remembering your communion with all that has been created, you can always take in moments of great beauty, astonishing joy, love without bounds, the brilliance of the smallest flowers, and the unbelievable wonder of our sunsets. It is right and fitting that we all give thanks and bow in gratitude. It is also good to assess those areas that may have been problematic, to take responsibility for what you did that was not of the highest, and then to set intentions for course correction in the future. In doing this each night, your subconscious is activated to support your intention as you sleep. Here is the prayer that I offered as I was writing this book:

> *At the end of this day, I am so incredibly happy. I understand how much grace has led me to the completion of these words. A thousand thanks, for the words of this book, for the growth I have attained to be able to write them, and for what will follow from this point forward as the book makes its way into the world. I also thank You, our Radiant Mother, for the clear beauty of this day. It astounds me after so many gray days. I thank you for the amazing healing that has taken place, and for my friends who were instrumental in this. I thank you for it all. I deeply bow to You in great gratitude,*
> *Namaste*

SEEING BEYOND INTO GREATER POSSIBILITIES

One of our great lessons in this life is learning to let go of our personal agendas regarding others and ourselves. When we expect that certain things must happen, we are acting from an ego state of self-importance rather than surrendering and accepting that there is a larger and greater power at play in our lives and in the universe. We are not all-knowing. We cannot presume to know what is best for another person at his or her highest soul level, and, despite our best attempts, we are not in control of certain situations. Things will play themselves out in a different and higher order than we could foresee. This is where we accept, trust, ask to see clearly, and open to grace filled possibilities.

Just as we learned that it is helpful to repeat a mantra during our everyday tasks, prayer can become more a part of our daily lives. We can pray at the beginning of an activity and at the end. Doing so keeps us centered and connected. This way we no longer see such tasks as mundane or boring. And, at the end of the day, we again connect to our Goddess selves with remembrance and thanksgiving for all the good of each day. Then we set a prayerful intention for the next day. When we live in this way, we are living in sanctified ways, breathing in that which is sacred, and sending our beautiful Goddess energies out into our world.

Prayer is heard even as a small thought. It is energy directed from us to another; however, we may want to go beyond our minds and thoughts into our bodies and our hearts to expand ourselves as much as possible. Just the acts of participating in such expansion open us in untold ways. Now is the time to believe in the power of your prayer. It is for this that you are here at this time. Remember... you are never alone.

Elaine Hoem

CONTEMPLATION

Here are three prayerful practices:

Center yourself and imagine your mind and your heart connected as one sacred energy so that you create a soulful connection and so that your prayers are infused with love.

1. Practice writing one of the above prayers for yourself or someone else. Then enlarge your prayer by praying for all people who suffer in this way. Make it all-encompassing by praying that all people everywhere be healed.

2. Take some time to center yourself, connecting your mind with your heart.
Write your larger prayer to express all that is vital to you.

Now embody your prayer by standing strong, grounded, and open. Name your prayer aloud with as much soulfulness as possible. You may want to add movement so that you are dancing your prayerful intention. Let each such step strengthen your prayer and your intention.

3. When you feel distressed by a world situation, pray for the perpetrators, the victims, the devastation, and for all those who help to right the situation. Also, pray for those who know they should speak out but have been afraid to do so. Pray for all others throughout the world who are affected, asking that the highest good be manifest for all involved, including yourself.

PART V

WAYS OF LOVING

CHAPTER 21

EVERYDAY LOVE STORIES

My Beloved,

It is my deep pleasure to speak to you of Love. I hope that you have experienced many forms of love in your life—the love of the other, the love of the mother and father, the love that you offer to a child—and then have this love reflected to you. There is the love that you know when you serve others when a homeless person bows to you because you helped him survive, the love of a friend who listens and helps you to heal. There are myriad forms of loving. Every way of loving is a form of grace. Moreover, always there is more. When you open to Me and allow Me to enter you, miracles of loving are created in each moment. I want you to know these ways. They are boundless. They touch the realm of angels and the golden beauty of the Divine. You may find them in the slightest touch of one person. You know these realms as you have known them before, in this life and previous ones. You long to experience them again. Open, see and embrace all the love that you find in all. Such love may leave you speechless. My love is all around you and surrounding you. It is easier to find when your mind is still, and your heart is open. This abundance of loving is your birthright. It is your true home. When you find Me in your everyday world, you have come home to your Sacred Self. This is my blessing. This is grace.

I invite you to read these Everyday Love Stories. Then take some time to contemplate your own Everyday Love Stories. They happen all around us. I am sure you will find interesting and diverse stories running through your life just as I did.

THE WARM COAT

A friend told me this story after just witnessing this scene. It is a cold wintery day in our city. There is a woman, possibly homeless, sitting on a curb and shivering. A car pulls up beside her. Another woman gets out and wraps a warm coat around the woman on the curb. These two women exchange a few words. One woman hugs the other. Love and goodness come in the form of a hug and a winter coat. The one woman drives away; the other is warmer in her heart and protected from the cold. This is agape. This is love.

THE CIRCLE OF DOVES

A fierce storm brings flooding and high winds that take down trees comes to the city in which I live. It is December and very cold. My underground oil tank contained oil to heat my house floods. There is no heat and I have children at home. I had my house listed for sale but now the yard is filled with downed tree branches and debris, making it looks like a disaster area. I am bereft and overwhelmed. I do not know where to start with all the cleanups.

Coming home from work one evening amid such chaos, I look out the front windows. In the middle of the cold, grey, icy street, there is a perfect circle of twelve large, plump, and luminous white doves, quiet, and very still. They seem to be holding space for me. Really? In ordinary reality, these things do not happen. There are no plump white doves in this town, especially in the middle of winter, yet here they are right in front of me. I know that this is a blessing, a gift, and a message to trust that something greater will come my way. I am humbled, and my frustration falls away. Over time, things right themselves with my home. We have a new and functioning furnace, and our lives move on in ordinary ways.

Later I reflect on the symbolism of doves in Judaism, Christianity, and Greek Antiquity. Doves signify peace universally. They bring hope and the proof of land sighted back to Noah. They signify new beginnings and in Judaism, the spirit of God. In ancient mythology, doves are significant to the Goddesses. Ishtar, Inanna, and Aphrodite are all depicted with doves.

When such otherworldly gifts are given, it is easy to honor the energies of Divine Providence and fall into a state of grace and gratefulness. This happened many years ago, yet I have never forgotten the gift of the pristine beauty of this circle of doves.

AWAKENING INTO WHOLENESS

A woman, broken by an abusive childhood comes to therapy. She is defended and angry. She casts others out. She holds recalcitrant messages of self-hatred and worthlessness. She believes her life cannot be changed and defies me "to make her better." The therapy takes some time. It is a gentle and confrontational process, sometimes difficult for both of us. At times, we laugh and sometimes cry. There are moments of hopefulness and remembrances of positive experiences that have built parts of her character that are quite wonderful. These qualities grow, session by session, as she settles into a truer sense of who she is.

Over time, she makes changes by leaving an abusive relationship and by beginning to develop positive friendships and activities that uplift who she is. She sets necessary boundaries with those who have abused her. Eventually, she is less broken, reactive, angry, and defensive. As the therapy progresses, she commits to herself in greater ways than ever before, taking care of her body with diet and the practice of yoga, joining others on a spiritual retreat, writing in a journal, and analyzing her dreams. Not every day is easy, great, or beautiful. There are times when she lapses into the self-hatred and anger of her old ways. During these times, she becomes very discouraged, but her strength and ability to see more clearly are in place. From here, she reorients her life and continues to move towards wholeness. This is hard therapeutic work. This is love.

Elaine Hoem

⁓

NAMASTE

I honor the place in you
In which the entire universe dwells.
It is a place of love, of light, of truth, and of peace.
When you are in that place in you
And I am in that place in me,
We are one.

This traditional East Indian greeting made its way to the Western world in the '60s with the yogis and gurus from India who brought meditative practices to the West. These words are full of meaning of the highest order. Each time we place our hands in prayer position over our hearts and bow to another, or ourselves, we are honoring that person and the God/Goddess dwelling within each of us. I use this blessing, this hallowed greeting before I lead any group activity. Immediately the energy in the room shifts, we all become quiet, our minds ease, and then we are more open to whatever will take place.

As I go about my day, I often practice this Namaste ritual by bowing internally, wishing another well—a homeless person, the driver next to me, or a friend I have not seen for a while. Or I bow to honor a thing of beauty that rises into my awareness—the new blooming rose, a beautiful bird, the sun rising brilliantly orange through the smoky day.

This is a soulful practice. It opens the heart to deepen our knowledge of the other as ourselves. It is a way to remember our communion with the natural world, a way of instilling peace within, and a way of expanding out in joy. In my community, more people are using this greeting so more people are being deeply honored. This is a small step yet a great way to change our world, one person at a time.

⁓

YOU DON'T KNOW HOW MUCH I LOVE YOU

I began the meditation practice I have today over 30 years ago. One of its main teachers left his body years before. One night, some years after I had been on this path, this great and powerful being from India, whom I had never met, came to me in a dream. It was short, clear, and strong. His message to me was, "You don't know how much I love you." I was humbled and awe-struck. I still am, to this day. I continue connecting with his loving presence daily and I commit to serving his yoga in my work and this writing.

MORE AND MORE LOVE

This is a story about the impact of our language, in this case, for the good. It is quite simple yet profound. One of my friends signs an email "More and more love." These words define who she always is. The gift of her four words reaches across hundreds of miles. In response, I slow down. I open and remember her loving ways. I appreciate her words and become more soulful, introspective, and grateful. Knowing of her great love sets the tone for the rest of my day. With this reminder, I choose only loving words as I share with others throughout my day. Such a simple act changes our inner state and our world.

17,282 TEEN AMBASSADORS

Between 2015 and 2017, 17,282 teens traveled from their homes throughout the world to live with other families around the world for both short-term and one-year exchanges through the Rotary International program for teen travel. This well-designed program has been in place since 1927. The teens receive training to be goodwill ambassadors for their home country. They are emissaries of peace.

These teens have courage, enthusiasm, and a sense of diplomacy as they represent their home country. They also have a heightened sense of adventure. They live in a new country with host families who open their homes to them as one of their children. They travel, learn, and play. Along the way, they learn another language, they realize their similarities to people of different cultures, and they participate in what their new country has to offer. In these months abroad, they grow into a fuller, expanded sense of who they truly are. When they return to their home country, they know themselves more clearly. Previous teen angst falls away. They educate others. Often, the families and friends from the "foreign countries" become part of their extended family for life. These young people become global citizens. Their world holds limitless possibilities for them. Because of this program, many more of us around the world connect with our brothers and sisters in other countries in more real and intimate ways. In this way, we no longer see people from other countries as "foreign," or people to fear. We grow in a sense of the possibilities of universal peace, and our families grow larger. We find that we have brothers, sisters, parents, and grandparents everywhere. This is worldwide generosity, and this is love.

TRAVELING WITH THE DIVINE FEMININE

A few years ago, I had a lengthy and serious illness. For a time, I was in and out of emergency rooms and hospital stays. I was not sure I would recover. One night, though, I had a dream. In the dream, I am getting ready to travel to the Oregon coast. My teacher appears, dressed in jeans instead of her usual flowing robes. She tells me that she will be with me during this journey. This means the world to me in my fear and brokenness. Her energy is palpable.

Such healing and loving energy can transform anything. Over time, this is exactly what happened. Over time, my body/mind/spirit healed and my life became vibrant once again.

This is the Divine Feminine in a form I recognize. She comes to aid and support me during times of distress and disease. Her presence assists in my shifting the lesser fearful perspectives I am carrying. It opens me to trust the larger story of my life and to remember and honor the grace always given to me and all of us. In the presence of Her grace, gradually I recover and start seeing myself as a vital person once again.

Elaine Hoem

CONTEMPLATION

What are your Everyday Love Stories? Write them in your journal to honor them. You might want to share them with a partner and/ or a trusted friend and ask to hear their stories as well.

What are your most soulful ways to open more deeply to others?

As your days go by, continue to note your Everyday Love Stories, writing them and sharing them. This is a practice in grace-filled remembrance.

CHAPTER 22

UNDOING ANCIENT BELIEFS AND
RELEASING OLD KARMA

Once we are on a spiritual path, we move from our smaller selves and contracted, ordinary ways of being into states of expansion and larger possibilities about ourselves and our world, and then back again. This is one of the essential soul dances in our being human. When we live in our everyday smaller world and feel spiritually disconnected, we live with worry, anxiety, attempts to control, and a sense of doer-ship that can overtake our best intentions. We may get many things done, but at a cost to our more soul-filled ways of living. The cost is often a lack of joy, spontaneity, and creativity. Loving oneself may be one of the most difficult parts of the journey of this life because our early conditioning to see ourselves as faulty and unworthy programmed so many of us. To become whole, it is necessary to uproot prolonged karmic, genetic, and familial programming. Unless we already have done sufficient self-exploration and healed our wounded parts, we may be consumed with self-blame and shame over supposed "sins" from our younger days. We also might resort to addictive behaviors to try to cope. Through the addiction, we experience temporary states of release, perhaps, but no true release.

When we move beyond our ego-based selves, we enter a completely different space. This new realm is one of grace, a sense of oneness, ease, and purity that brings us home to our higher and more connected Selves. Once we know this state, we will long to return to it again and again. This longing sets us on a spiritual path and a greater commitment to ourselves to grow into a state of Oneness. It is in this search that we awaken to act in ways that expand upon our karma and our destiny. Otherwise, we are caught in karmic conditioning and do not grow into our true possibilities.

When we live less consciously, we continue to play out the negative messages that came from our past. These can be so ingrained that they are a constant and sometimes daily part of us. We would not even recognize ourselves without them. These messages fill our minds from the words and behaviors of others who lived in his or her own self-destructive and less conscious ways. They cause great wounding. They are negative distortions that are not reflective of the truth of a person's beautiful, untainted soul. It is imperative that those of us on spiritual paths uproot and excise these negative karmic conditions and then replace them with loving, soothing, and truthful thoughts. These new thoughts bring us into harmony with that which is of a loving and higher truth. When we inhabit these serene states, we have more energy, more to give to our families and community, and more strength of character in any situation.

I know that it is not easy to make these shifts. The work can be difficult particularly as we envision a seemingly long road ahead; however, this road is an essential one to take. It offers us the possibility of releasing past roadblocks so that we can more readily open to our higher selves. Being on a spiritual path itself allows grace, Divine support, and love to step alongside us for assistance. Relationship, medical, and psychological crises may occur that shake us into exploring more than we previously have been.

Whatever happens to wake us up, whatever it takes to set us on a spiritual path is great news because we now begin to make a break with the wounding from our past. We can embark on a commitment to self-discovery that changes everything. It is in these shifts of focus that everything about us can become clearer and lighter, healed, and whole, and once we are whole psychologically and spiritually, we have more to offer to others.

We are here to undo our dark and stuck places by learning to step out of our wounding, to look deeply into how we are made in terms of family dynamics, karma, and our dharma. And, as our understanding increases, we know that we are meant to rise above all wounding to become as great as possible in how we live and in how we share our love.

When we stay silent, our wisdom, intuition, and highest Self go underground. In childhood, it may not have been safe to be who we were and certainly not safe to have a voice or express an opinion.

Silence in such households becomes deadly. Often the person who is the loudest, or the angriest, or the most abusive has a voice. And this usually is not the child. The child becomes still and seemingly unknowing until something occurs to wake him or her up. It could be the touch of an angel or a vision of the Mother or the light of Her Son. It could be the compassion of a teacher or the urging of a coach that opens a new sense of what is possible. The gentle stillness of nature or the surprising awe of seeing a double rainbow for the first time may provide a sense of safety and comfort that previously had been unavailable. Anything or anyone could set in motion a wake-up call from the Mother giving us a message we cannot miss.

It says *"Awaken. It is time, and here is the next step of the path to follow."*

We may need the help of psychodynamic therapists, energy workers, or others who heal and who honor the holistic beings that we are. These guides can help us unravel and heal the traumas that have kept us bound. It takes courage to embark upon a journey that brings us greater insight into ourselves and others.

We all have shadow sides that we cannot always see, so we sometimes need the wise, listening ears of a well-trained person to point out what we are missing. Such deep and compassionate support allows us to move carefully, cautiously, and lovingly into the painful places that our shadow sides represent to help us learn new truths about who we are on the other side of our wounding. We enter the process of psychotherapy to become free and clear of all kinds of trauma and karma. Once we have healed, we find that this work is worth everything. We can open more and more to the truth of our soul-filled Selves. In the process, we each find our true home. As we look deeply into our past and can see others and ourselves more clearly, we will be able to offer forgiveness, to ourselves and others. True and deep forgiveness opens us further into states of grace. Then the tendrils of grace reach out to touch others who have been involved. The reverse is also true. When we hold onto judgments, anger, and resentments, we are ego-bound and unable to move further into more expansive states of being.

When we begin to explore the past experiences that have caused us to lock up inside, we often find that they lead us back to childhood and the wounding that happened then. One thing I know to be true is that if we all knew back then what we know today, it would be easier to understand and forgive our younger selves. At that time in our lives, we were doing the absolute best that we could to survive difficult and soul-damaging situations by making use of the information that was available to us with only a child's awareness to understand it. We must lessen the blame that we attach to our younger selves and instead honor and support the child self so that we can free that part of us from shame and self-criticism. When we hold onto those "wrongs" that we committed as children, ways that we now feel go against our adult values and beliefs about who we truly are, we are only hurting ourselves and perhaps others. A better choice would be to practice self-forgiveness for our child self. And then, we can address our highest intentions of today by consecrating ourselves to act with integrity, greater self-awareness, and wisdom in the present and future. Doing so frees us from continuing to carry blame, guilt, and shame.

Yet, forgiving our younger selves or even our older selves and others is not a simple or easy thing. At times, hearing about a horrific event that happened to someone in childhood that was only quite recently remembered or that kind of event that happened more recently, we hear the person saying, "I have forgiven him or her." There is no doubt that this kind of forgiveness, a forgiveness that is based on true agape love, *is* possible. This act of immediate forgiveness is the act of one who is living in the knowledge of All That Is, an intimate relationship with the Divine. However, it has been my experience as a psychotherapist, and in my own life, that immediate or near immediate response of forgiveness probably comes from our sense of needing to say the right thing that we believe needs to be said. For most of us, true forgiveness happens over time. A psychological and spiritual process takes place with sufficient self-reflection and healing. During this process, understanding and compassion for our younger selves will evolve and lead to enhanced visions for all concerned.

To arrive at this place, we first must let go of anger, self-hatred, negative self-talk, deep sadness, and resentment towards ourselves and towards those who have harmed us. This is not quick or easy work; however, it is a vital pathway. Lack of forgiveness keeps us stuck in judgments, grudges, guilt, a need to be in control at all costs, and the incapacity to understand karmic situations at more expanded levels. All these ways are ego-based. They keep our defenses locked in place, our negative egos intact, and our longing for spiritual connections at bay. If there is no forgiveness, we continue to carry judgment and a sense of self-righteousness that bind us to the ego. This creates a sense of separation that fuels our unwillingness to let go of control. Inner child therapy with a skilled therapist who can help you look at your child self is a valuable and beautiful way to heal such wounds.

When we have grown in our ability to understand the larger picture of why things happened as they did, we may find that we all are capable of egregious harm to others, perhaps earlier in this life or past ones. When we can forgive ourselves and step into others' shoes in this way, our defenses fall away so that empathy and compassion become a part of who we are. These two spiritual qualities enhance our understanding of both ourselves and others. It is only then that we forgive from our minds, hearts, and emotions. Gentleness towards ourselves and an acceptance of others become our constant life choice, and this frees us from the burdens of the past.

When you recognize that you are stuck in ways that no longer work, seek the greatest help possible. Then do not hold back. Move beyond your fear and learn to access your deepest wisdom. You will receive blessings for doing your soul work. Eventually, you will understand who you are from a much higher perspective. Then you will be able to honor your life as it is and celebrate who you have become.

CONTEMPLATION

Please spend some time writing in your journal about childhood traumas that may be causing you pain in the present.

What kind of healing work have you already done?

What are the results?

What needs to be forgiven?

Within yourself?

For another?

What are the next steps you will take to become free of this karma?

CHAPTER 23

NAMING AND RELEASING FALSE GODS

I call addictions false gods because of the inordinate time, energy, and attention we give to them, and because of all the time, energy, and attention, they take from us. When our vital energies align with an addiction, we live in lesser states of being. Addiction casts a pall over us so that we no longer can see clearly. When an addiction needs to be satisfied, it becomes far more important than anything else. We often neglect or completely ignore our primary relationships and the daily routines that are so essential to a well-lived and more conscious life. The powerful pull of addiction has a very real and strong life of its own. It can completely overtake our personality, our mental, emotional, and physical health, and, in fact, our whole way of being. Overall, addictions take us away from our spiritual essence, which often results in movement in directions that lead us down false paths or in no direction at all. Like a moth drawn irrevocably towards a flame, the addict is drawn toward his or her chosen addiction, the false god, which appears so attractive even though in just a matter of time, a horrible conflagration is guaranteed to take place.

An addiction is a misdirected pattern. There is falseness contained in addictive behavior; its roots are in the act of denial. How often have we heard or read of someone saying, "No, I don't have a problem" and then declaring any number of excuses as to why what he or she is doing is not a problem. Perhaps you have heard yourself making those same sorts of excuses as well. When we honor the false gods, our eyes and hearts close to the brilliance and goodness that surround us. The great sadness in all of this is that we cannot see what we cannot see despite messages from loved ones about what is happening.

~

Nearly all of us have at least one addiction, sometimes several. Alcohol, drugs, and pornography are ones that we often think of first when we hear the word "addiction." But the truth is that just about anything we do that has ongoing and overpowering control over our freedom is an addiction. There are many possible candidates: food, work, relationships, suffering, money, power, drama, victimization, computers, tweeting, perfectionism, phones, guns, shopping, video games, Facebook, sex, and gambling. You might know of others.

Newer addictions have been born out of our ever-growing dependence on technology. Such addictions are more difficult to name and to admit to because of the immense benefits we derive from our technology. Our schooling and our work are often completely dependent upon their usage. People young and older spend all hours of the day and night connected to computers and phones, often at the expense of quality time for themselves and those they love. It takes a good deal of soul searching to know when to take a break—when to put the phone down and engage in conversation with the people who are right in front of us.

Addictions keep us locked in behaviors that ensure that we will drop farther and farther away from the lighted Selves that we are. Addictions often start with positive intentions, and even with the search for God. However, we end up immersing ourselves in the realms of an underbelly that has immediate seductive attraction. The addictive habits temporarily allow us to forget our depression, our boredom, our pain, and our seeming inability to foster change within ourselves. We stay blanketed in a lack of awareness and a lesser consciousness. The addiction keeps us from seeing and sensing what we know to be true about ourselves.

> *Several years ago, I had a most wonderful friend. He often lived in a state of wonder and beauty. From him, I learned about the spiritual journey, about creating beauty around me, and about loving ways of being. These ways set the stage for who I am today. I am sharing a little of his story as an example of how the longing for God can lead to addictive experiences. It is a cautionary tale. I also am sharing it in honor of him.*
>
> *When my friend was in his early 20s, he experimented with psychedelic drugs and was enthralled by the experiences, the spiritual insights he received, and how his reality expanded to include the numinous. For some time, these experiences seemed to enhance his ordinary life.*
>
> *Over the years, however, he added other drugs and copious amounts of alcohol to his days. When I would tell him of my concerns, his response was "This is what people in my world do." He was unable to see these choices as habits that had become addictive; nor could he see how they were harming him. Instead, his use of drugs and the addition of alcohol had become attempts to deal with stressors in his life and had given him an entrée into a certain kind of social life. Over time, he devolved further into addictive ways, becoming angry and critical, less present, and less able to love.*
>
> *Eventually, his body succumbed to the years of abuse. Those of us who loved him were left with large holes in our hearts, missing such a beautiful man, and the wonder, goodness, and grace he brought to our lives.*

Addictions may not become consciously visible until a person is in his or her late teens or early twenties or older. However, they often begin long before that. When we take addictions back to their source, we find that the antecedents often come from the distorted beliefs and wounding that existed in our families of origin, or from traumatic events that occurred at other times in our lives. When we do not get our primary and rightful needs met by our parents and caretakers, or when we are traumatized by the acts of other people or events later in our lives, we consciously and subconsciously look to something else for ease and fulfillment. This fulfillment might be found in people, material objects, or situations that exhibit qualities that are similar to or in direct contrast to the qualities that were either lacking or in overabundance during childhood. For example, a daughter who has a mother who is overwhelmingly rigid regarding food and eating habits may develop an eating disorder in which she seems to have complete self-control despite her mother's urging and anger for her to eat.

When addiction is a part of a person's life, he or she is driven to a greater or lesser extent to try to fill the body, heart, and soul with an antidote to that which was absent or distorted earlier in life. If, and when, a person recognizes the addiction for what it is, hopefully, he or she will seek ways to address the problem. However, we usually are not able to heal serious addictions on our own. This is true because once we are mired in the chronic patterns of addictive behaviors, we cannot address what we cannot see on our own. Good recovery programs provide the first order of recovery by shifting the relationship away from the false gods so that the addicted person can reclaim his or her truer Self. They help the person deal with the addiction as it is in the present, through strength of will, community support, and behavioral programs. And these changes in behavior are a necessary first step.

While these recovery programs can be successful on their own, many of them do not focus on the origin of the addiction. Once a strong pattern of recovery is in place, what must be added is counseling that will lead the person to the origins of this lifestyle choice so that he or she can face and address the root causes of the addiction.

I recommend psychotherapy to discover and heal the psychological wounds we carry from our past, which are the root causes of psychological disorders and/or addictions. Along the way, we must also heal the spirit.

Spiritual growth is dependent upon real soul searching. Once we see, feel, and understand these problems, we can release and heal them. Then real spiritual growth can begin.

It is important to note that there can be a misstep at this point of the recovery. Some people move from a general recovery program directly into spiritual practices without the necessary supports in place. These practices on their own may not be enough to affect the kind of changes in the quality of our lives and our relationships that we are seeking. To be whole, we must do *such* difficult work.

Images and memories may come forth that require a person to look at past antecedents, to own the traumas associated with them, and then engage in healing work with its concomitant release. This can be challenging work, which is why it is wise to be working with a professional therapist who understands the intimate connection between psychological healing and the spirit. Compassionate psychotherapy helps us unwind our previous traumas, view them in transparent and soul-defining ways, and then helps us clear and heal the karma and traumas related to them. This work assists us in moving beyond the traumas, in finding the essential lessons contained within such experiences, and then to move forward with our lives in more grace-filled ways. Such inner work also shifts karmic energies from our lineage and frees our children from being burdened as we were.

Without such treatment, those of us who struggle with addictive behaviors will most likely continue to act impulsively to fulfill our desires. In the process, we forget our search and our deeper longing for spiritual experiences due to the presence of an addictive haze. Despite the desires and promises we make to ourselves to change, the vital energies we use to chase an addiction will never lead us home. In fact, the longer we serve the false gods and the longer we fail to admit to our addictions, the more difficult it is to step away from them. In this case, it is often just a matter of time before some sort of crisis implodes or explodes to completely change our usual pattern. If we survive, we have a choice. Hopefully, we choose to pull ourselves out of the addictive mire and the den of the false gods and begin our search for our truer Selves. It is then that we have a greater chance of returning to our spiritual home.

The good news is that once we have chosen to walk a spiritual path, the attention and commitment we give to our new journey will gradually lessen the power of the false gods, allowing us the energy to find the joy that we had hoped to find through our addictive behaviors. This time, though, the joy comes from living a more wholesome and holy life.

This does not mean that we are home free. This is a process. These shifts often take us back into the old and then out again into the new. Therefore, it is not uncommon to realize that we have unconsciously fallen back into addictive behaviors. This can happen more than once until newer patterns that are more positive are securely in place. However, there is no need to lose heart: once we gain more and more of the newer and deeper perspectives that bring greater value to our lives, we are less tempted to return to the addictive path. Then the original commitment we created through that first step in a recovery process becomes stronger so that once again we move forward on the journey to our higher Self.

Once we decide to make new commitments to ourselves, to become all we can be, we can consecrate that intention by making a vow to realign with our Soul's purpose. To strengthen this vow, we make it from both our minds and our hearts. Doing so takes our intention to the level of the sacred. This is especially important to contemplate, after having lived through addictive reasoning and actions, which do not attend to the sacred. Therefore, this is a time, again and again, to devote our lives to our highest visions, to set clear intentions to rise to those visions, and to pray that the addictive patterns lessen so that we can evolve into people who live through their true soul dances.

Here are three vital questions for you to ask yourself if you are concerned about addiction in your life.

On a scale from 1 to 10, with 1 being a minor addiction and 10 the most severe addiction, what number would you give to your addictive concern?

Are others concerned about you and an addiction? Do they talk to you about their concerns? What are your responses?

Often a person with an addiction will be in denial, saying things like "Quit worrying about me. I am fine." or "Leave me alone. I know what I am doing." Are you using those kinds of responses?

An additional way to give yourself more information about a pattern of this nature in your life is to give up the pattern completely for 30 days. There are two provisos for this exercise.

FIRST: DO NOT ATTEMPT THIS EXERCISE ON YOUR OWN WITHOUT PROPER MEDICAL AND PSYCHOLOGICAL OVERSIGHT AND CARE IF YOU HAVE AN ADDICTION TO ALCOHOL, PHARMACEUTICAL DRUGS, OR STREET DRUGS.

Second: Initially commit yourself to abstinence for 30 days. Then re-evaluate. Knowing that you have chosen an end date for what may begin to feel like deprivation will help you stay with the exercise longer.

If you decide to try this exercise, at the end of 30 days, evaluate what you learned and how you feel. If you were unable to let the addictive pattern go, please look more deeply into this pattern and consider seeking help. You may have a more serious problem than you want to admit.

As you move forward on your new spiritual path, practices such as Hatha yoga, meditation, mantra repetition, journaling, and dreamwork provide wonderful support. They are also stabilizing adjuncts to psychotherapy. The more consciousness, honor, and love we bring into all parts of our lives and our body-mind connection, the greater our spiritual awakening. As we let go of self-limiting and self-destructive behaviors, we gain a greater capacity to practice forgiveness of ourselves and others. There is a huge relief in getting to the other side of our wounding. Enormous freedom becomes available at all levels of our being as we release early trauma and addictions. We become freer and freer, lighter, happier, and more loving.

CONTEMPLATION

Name your addiction/s.

Write about how they serve you.

Write what you feel about them.

Write what messages you tell yourself about them.

Are there changes you need to make in your life to shift focus from the addiction to your spiritual journey?

What support do you need?

Where will you reach out to get such support?

If you choose not to make changes at this time, write about why you are making this decision.

If you have overcome an addiction, write about the steps that you took to do so. These steps will be a guide towards making other shifts in your life as you move forward.

CHAPTER 24

IT IS TIME TO FORGIVE MYSELF

In our early lives, we often receive negative messages about who we are. One of the reasons we came to this lifetime is to resolve karmic problems that we continue to carry. Some of us have abusive backgrounds to overcome; some have been the abusers. Others have medical conditions that are difficult to manage. Some of us lived in situations at one time or another that caused PTSD symptoms and that continue to haunt and destabilize us. Despite our best efforts to repair and heal these traumas, we often find ourselves damaged physically and emotionally or with addictive behaviors that stop us in our tracks. We may have intense fear or anger towards others who have harmed us—then find it difficult or impossible to be trusting and open with others. Or we may continue to choose relationships that contain similar destructive patterns.

All this leads to living in ways that continue the damage. We relentlessly carry messages of unworthiness or messages that tell us that we are unable to control our lives—messages that still resound and rule even though the person who originally harmed us in these ways may be long gone. We look in the mirror and find ourselves less than adequate. We may feel incapable of performing daily tasks at home and work. We tell ourselves that we are not as good as, as pretty as, as talented as _____ (most of us can fill in the blank). Our inner messages continually reinforce such negative self-talk. We are stuck. Some of us live out a lifetime, or even more than one lifetime, in these ways.

As we live our lives with these messages ingrained within, they discolor our ways of being in relationships within our families and with others. We unconsciously play out patterns from our families of origins that set the stage to hold these messages of our unworthiness, inadequacies, and guilt in place. To "prove" our feelings of lack, we often act outwardly in certain ways that recreate patterns that seem wrong and immoral deep inside. We are guilt-laden because they collide with our best values and beliefs. As a result, we continue to beat ourselves up, hide the darker parts of who we are, and pretend that all is fine. Within, we are living in turmoil, shame, depression, and anxiety; outwardly, we may be living with an addiction. We may want and need to hide from the world. *Enormous* energy goes into maintaining these defenses. Spiritual progress is blocked.

Once we can bring all this to consciousness, we wake up to our true essence. We become aware. We connect our past and our present ways of living. We understand that the traumatic events of our lives have been necessary to foster our growth in our soul's journey. After we have healed such woundedness, we become alive and free enough to become open and, yes, even vulnerable. All these qualities working together grant us the ability to make conscious choices. The practice of forgiveness of oneself and others can arise from this gift, a sure sign that we are moving steadily on the path of All That Is.

> *Long ago, I had the opportunity to work with a woman who was sexually abused as a child. In many ways, as an adult, she had not been able to move beyond the trauma. While in therapy, we had an experience of her being in a light trance and getting in touch with her wounded child self. At first, her little one was needy. She clung to my client and wanted my client, her grown self, to hold her tight, which my client did while giving her inner child affirming and healing messages. After a time, when her child-self felt safe and supported, she bounded off my client's lap and was off to play and dance, perfectly healed at this moment.*

If you do not yet know your own beauty, following a spiritual path will take you across the chasms that your ego and karma have created over lifetimes. With spiritual awareness and constancy as you grow towards that which is sacred, you will come out on the other side. It is there that you will find your beauty and your magnificence.

The following meditation is one you will want to practice as different aspects of your past become evident. Each time you practice this meditation, you probably will notice a lightening, a sense of calmness, and a deeper sense of understanding. With each practice of this meditation, you are releasing old patterns and karma from the past that no longer serve you.

SELF-FORGIVENESS MEDITATION

Please follow the link below or scan the QR code below. It links you to www.everydaysouldances.com/meditations.

CONTEMPLATION

Write about your experience with this meditation. How will you continue to access the energies of your Higher Self?

Are there other parts of your life that are calling for self-forgiveness?

Practice writing and remembering positive affirmations about who you truly are on your spiritual journey and the mantra HAM SA. Write as many positive statements to yourself as possible.

I am _____. HAM SA.

I am _____. HAM SA.

I am _____. HAM SA

CHAPTER 25

TAKING EXQUISITE CARE OF YOURSELF

When we embark upon the spiritual journey, we are playing in the fields of the dichotomy of ego and spirit. This yogic dance is about letting go of the small, stressful, and ego-bound ways that attempt to control and judge both others and ourselves. Once we move into more enhanced and lighted ways of being in which the ego is in service to the higher Self, there is an opening, an awakening, an "a-ha" moment as our lives become more enlightened ones. The ego-bound patterns drop away, and we release attachments to those habits that have kept us bound. This takes awareness and practice, constancy and courage, and the willingness to correct course. Perhaps your heart will open in falling in love with a baby, a remembrance of a first love, or a feeling of unconditional love.

One of the most important outgrowths of such inner work is that it brings us to a higher state of being, a more enlightened state of understanding to all our relationships. Our families and the people of the world benefit greatly from any of these changes.

Once we have the experiences of cosmic consciousness moving through us and within us, we want to, even yearn to move gracefully from a sense of limitation into the limitless remembrance of our infinite state of being. We learn to reside more and more in our expanded sense of Self. There are two parts to this dance. The first is to say "No" to old, worn-out, negative states and the people whose ways have kept us stuck or have limited us in our growth. Releasing these old mannerisms that have contributed to our stockpile of negative karma allows for the quiet and clarity of spiritual understanding to enter. We now can enlarge our understanding as our consciousness deepens and our compassion for others and ourselves increases. Most of these shifts are shifts in awareness that allow for small and potent changes in our being.

The list of suggested actions given below are contemplations to help you practice new ways. They are simple ideas with profound results when we take them in fully. Each one is a brilliant jewel, a gift to yourself. You might want to read the entire list and then focus on the one you would like to try. After choosing one practice, hold it close to your heart as you remember it throughout your next days. Allow it to evolve into a practice that grounds you in ways that strengthen both your sense of self and your love of Self. I recommend that you bring one suggestion into your life for at least the next week or so, remembering it often during each day. Ideally, you will practice one of these ways until it becomes habitual. Then, when you journal, write what you have observed and how you feel during and after playing with grace in this way.

When some of your favorite ways have become routine, you can add others. What we are doing with this practice is filling our consciousness with positive, expansive, and loving thoughts. Each time we pay attention to such thoughts, we become lighter and more astonished at the possibilities that we can create in our world. Some of the inner shifts you notice may be subtle changes in your state; however, your notice of such changes will reinforce your initial awareness. Each positive shift is worthy of your honor and attention. You might also create other practices that speak strongly to you.

Please take some time to contemplate and journal the best ways for you to expand your love of Self.

*

Find beauty and joy in all that you do, in the tasks of this day. Find sacredness in the simplest things.

*

Imagine opening your third eye and your heart chakra as well as your physical eyes. Expand your vision so that your physical eyes see in soft and far-seeing ways. Become quiet. Breathe slowly and deeply. Imagine your third eye and your energetic heart opening wide, taking in as much of life as possible.

What do you experience when you do this? Hold this opening throughout your day.

*

Practice sending loving thoughts to yourself and to all others you see today.

*

This day practice gentleness in touch, gentleness in seeing, and gentleness with your words.

*

Today, as you go about your day, practice the HAMSA mantra to be at one with the birds, the sky, with all others, and with yourself, saying I Am, I Am That. I Am at One with the sky. I Am at One with the meal I cook. I am at One with the people on the street. I am at One with the deep rest at the end of the day. I Am at One with It All. HAMSA.

*

Imagine living this day freely, easily, and joyfully. Then practice doing so. Pay attention to what you do to shift to a more lighthearted and fluid state.

*

Make each moment sacred by the quality of your attention.

*

Dance.

*

Chant and sing.

*

On this day notice the most precious, transformative, and vital moment. Honor it and contemplate it deeply. It is good to write about such experiences in your journal. On some days, you might find many such moments. Then you will know that you are dwelling in the hands of the Goddess, the Luminous One.

*

Name your intention for this day and then act on it. At the end of the day, contemplate what this was like for you. How do you take this practice further?

*

Clear your emotions and repetitive thoughts daily. Keep replacing such thoughts with the thought "I AM THAT" and the mantra HAMSA. For example, change "My grief has overtaken me today" to "I am grieving at this time, HAMSA." Then go on to what the next thing is that you notice. "I am the darkening skies this evening. HAMSA." "I am the forest as it enters into the darkness. HAMSA."

*

Expect nothing. Accept everything.

*

Ask, "Why am I feeling this way?" Allow the feeling to dissolve and breathe it back to the source. Later write about what you do to shift from a particular feeling to being At One and at peace.

*

Pay attention to what your intuition is telling you. What do you know to be true? Write about your intuition and your awareness and actions that they generate.

*

Trust that there is a reason for all that is happening. Be curious and open. Notice any answers that come to you.

*

Notice and be open to all the love that comes your way. Know that you are worthy. Practice living in this receptive state.

*

Take time to be in nature every day, if possible, and to become consciously at one with the natural world.

*

Even during difficult times, find moments that bring beauty, joy, and comfort to you.

*

Take time to be present in your body. Have fun with all the ways you can embody freedom, mystery, grace, and ecstasy through dance, song, sensuality, and sexuality.

*

Write about how you are developing your spiritual life.

*

Clear your repetitive thoughts each day through prayer. Ask that your perspective and perceptions be broadened with enhanced understanding.

*

Write about how you see yourself this day. Who are you from the perspective of your soul?

*

See a problem or a disagreeable person as a teacher rather than an enemy. What can you learn from this situation or person?

*

Talk to a wise person. Write about what you learn.

*

Say "Yes" to higher energy choices and "No" to ways of malaise, addictions, or other choices that take you down a negative path.

*

Go deeper in all areas of life – health, heart, diet, meditation, consciousness, relationships, loving, care of self, and loving care of others.

*

Create something that brings you joy.

*

Be as mindful as often as possible so that you are creating sacredness in each moment.

*

Find ways to simplify your life, and then do so, a little at a time.

*

Remember that you are more than your personality and your problems. Write about the dance between your ego and your spiritual Self. Then write about how to meld the two worlds into one joyous embrace.

*

Be loving, kind, and gentle in all your interactions with everyone.

*

Ask yourself "How best can I serve during this day?"

*

Set positive intentions for the next day before falling asleep then review them again before starting your next day.

*

Spend time in silence and then write about how becoming silent changes your state.

*

Practice bowing in Namaste internally to each person you meet this day—the people on the street, the people who pass you in their cars, the loved ones in your family, and the others at your job. See each person as an extension of the Divine Mother.

*

Get to know the people who serve you. Enjoy them. Compliment them. Thank them.

*

Remember there are many things you can do to heal yourself. What is a way you can practice this day?

RAINBOW MEDITATION

This meditation is deeply healing. When we bring colors into our being with intention, they infuse our subtle and physical bodies with color and light. These experiences release blockages and dis-ease at various levels of our being and infuse our being with colored light. This light flows into different parts of our being so that various organs, tissues, and cells receive exactly the light that they need for greater healing. This meditation is also an excellent way to make shifts from lesser states to higher ones.

Use the QR Code below to access the recording of this meditation on the Everyday Soul Dance website: <u>www. everydaysouldances.com/meditations</u>.

CONTEMPLATION

What happens within you and to you with others when you practice these ways?

Write about what you are doing to live a greater, more fulfilled life and how you will continue to practice self-loving ways.

PART VI

THE YOGA OF RELATIONSHIP

CHAPTER 26

OUR KARMA AND OUR LOVE

When we look at love from a karmic perspective, we understand that we come into families and create relationships to resolve negative karma, to grow in love, to serve others, and to find God/Goddess within each other and ourselves. In doing so, we create more karma that is positive and become soulful emissaries in service to our world. This is why we are here. We find that love is very fluid and that the energies of love transcend time and space. We also understand that love exists beyond our egos, blame, judgments, attempts to control another, and the need to be right. We come to know the broad breadth that love casts over us throughout our lifetimes despite our dependencies, depressions, anxieties, anger, addictions, and trauma. Once we can move through difficult karma in relationships and can view our lives with expanded vision, we will learn to honor and embrace both ourselves and others just as we all are. Through all the ways in which we love, we grow into a higher version of ourselves.

In the yoga of relationships, we move from the distortions that we carry—the shadow sides, the old familiar patterns, inherited or newly created, from our family patterns that were not of love— into the loving nurturance of others. This is the movement from conditional love to unconditional love and from self-centeredness into our most compassionate and loving ways of being.

This yoga is also the movement from distortions in communication to speech that communicates clarity, honesty, and constancy with all our words. As we move through and beyond these distortions, we learn what it means to love another, while maintaining a strong center within ourselves. As we pay more attention to who we are inside and who we are in relationships, we will find that our partners are not in our lives to make us whole. It is our responsibility alone to make ourselves whole, hopefully with a partner's support.

After the infatuation stage in a relationship inevitably subsides, there is a likelihood that problems will arise as we come face-to-face with our loved one's shadow sides and with the shadow sides within ourselves. This happens because relationships offer us the opportunity to hold up mirrors to each other so that each person can see parts of him or herself that would otherwise remain hidden. To grow in any of our relationships, we must look within to the parts we have not yet seen. This can be both surprising and troubling. When we acknowledge these previously unseen parts of ourselves, we can make positive shifts that allow us to grow emotionally and spiritually. Then we are doing our part in both the relationships with our loved ones and with ourselves by freeing ourselves from smaller needs and desires. When we commit to changing those habits and patterns, their numbers often diminish or disappear throughout a lifetime as we bring more spiritually enhanced parts of ourselves to all our relationships.

Our commitment to developing new understanding and new ways free us of past distortions, allowing us to rewrite our karma with such sacred acts. In this way, any relationship becomes a pathway to consecrated ways of living. In this newly experienced unconditional loving, we create more connection without hesitation. We know that our relationships foster awakenings for all the people involved. Often, we come to recognize the constant presence of miracles in our lives.

Each day, each of us has choices to make, to be selfish or selfless, to be gentle or aggressive, unfeeling, or loving. Our partners are our strong and ever-present teachers who show us who we are inside and who we are with others. To love well is to become very humble and aware. There are always many opportunities to honor or misuse, to communicate or to close down. We can bow deeply to our partners as our teachers as well as our lovers. Each day, we recommit to loving. This is the yoga of love and relationship. It draws us into our divinity within, and into our intimacy with others. Then the trials and gifts of loving become the yoga of our relationships.

One of the trials of creating a loving relationship is committing to first dive deep within to find a calm center of self-love so that we do not lose ourselves in any relationship. Love and infatuation are two quite different experiences. Infatuation wears thin after a time when excitement and sexual desires wane. Love extends beyond infatuation. To be the best possible partner involves a commitment to the other over time that includes a willingness to care for the other's spiritual growth along with a willingness to grow within ourselves. All of this gets complicated when we have not yet learned to love ourselves as well as we might love another. What we often define as love is often an immersion into ego-based ways of desire, neediness, a lack of appropriate boundaries, or attempts to fulfill less-conscious parts of ourselves through another. Clearing the way to recognize these false starts sometimes means that we move through various relationships. Each relationship, no matter its quality or its length, can be an excellent teacher about what love is and what it is not.

Because we live in societies in which we receive many negative messages about who we are and who we should be in relationships, it sometimes feels safer to close ourselves off to loving because of fear and lack of trust. We do so through anger, detachment, depression, and addictions. The negative ego has a great investment in protecting the status quo no matter the spiritual, physical, and emotional costs. We will stay ego-bound and locked into ways of being that deny and delay spiritual growth until we experience new opportunities for shifts in awareness. To love deeply and well means confronting our fears of loving and allowing love in. It means that we grow into knowing that we are worthy of love and of being loved. It is no easy task to achieve this, and it may take a lifetime, or even several, to achieve. However, we can still take the next steps along the way.

We know we have moved beyond fear when we can stay in the presence of love without running away or collapsing. This means learning and deepening our communication skills when love becomes problematic. This means moving beyond the dysfunctional patterns we learned about relationships from our families. It means giving up old beliefs about our lack of worthiness regarding love. Such growth changes and enhances our destiny.

Eventually, as we grow in the art of relationship and as we desire spiritual connection, we will long for intimacy and connections that are more meaningful. Here too we need to pause and consciously address the issues that arise. From the earlier pages in this book, we know that we bring karmic imprints, values, beliefs, and wounds

205

from our parents, families, and cultures into our relationships. We may carry childhood traumas within that set a stage upon which both partners will play out karma that is destined to happen in this lifetime. We are mirrors for each other—guides and teachers. If we carry shadow sides, and most of us do, they too are part of our relationship with our partners and their shadow selves. This is often treacherous territory to navigate until we become more conscious.

The yogic dance of relationship means that we figure out this dichotomy between longing for spiritual connection in our relationships and being too afraid to have such connection. When there are ruptures in loving, it is not only two people who suffer; it involves many as such sadness affects our entire community. This is because the losses are pervasive and because they cut so broadly and so deeply. While some relationships must end for a variety of reasons, at the level of the soul, all relationships endure through lifetimes, or at least until all karma between two people is resolved. We can close gateways to a relationship in personal reality for this lifetime, but soul love endures well beyond. It seems clear to me that any time we can heal a troubled relationship, it is of the highest order to do so.

When two people are blocked with negative emotions and behaviors, marital therapy is in order so that a wise and well-trained third person can see and name the dynamics and distortions. The couple then has opportunities to practice new ways of communicating and acting, correcting distortions, and becoming more loving and compassionate with each other. Over time, with renewed commitment, it is possible to practice more refined states of love. The relationship heals and transforms. We can honor our partners and ourselves for moving further into love. Each time this happens, negative karma gets resolved, and our loving uplifts us and by extension those around us.

It is also true that in some situations, the healing will happen by setting necessary boundaries and moving on. Your karma and the other's may coincide for a time—short or long. We do not necessarily know. There is a time for people to come together, and a time for letting go. When a consciously held relationship is truly over, both partners can find peace. It will be clear. There will be an absence of energy, anger, obsession, anxiety, and wishing that things could be different. There will be a sense of equanimity within you regarding the other person. When this is evident, you know that you have done the necessary healing work. Again, having the help of an accomplished therapist will move the process of letting go along.

There is, of course, another side to the ending of a relationship. When there are problems, and one or both of us stay the same, relationships deteriorate, and the connections become tainted. Learning and soul growth are thwarted. When this happens, we can find other ways to grow and, perhaps, further learning will happen in another relationship or another lifetime. However, while we can hope for shifts towards greater and deeper communication, this does not always happen. Some people are unable to go further; it is not their karma or destiny to do so. Others refuse—often out of fear of letting love in, from addiction, from a lifetime of detachment, or trauma. In others, there is so much brokenness from past family dynamics and previous karma that people stay stuck in ways that seem unproductive and less conscious.

One of the more difficult dynamics in a relationship is one in which two people are co-dependent upon each other. Co-dependency is a distortion, a misguided view of who we are with each other. Co-dependency means, "I will forego what is right, best, and of the highest good for me to try to make sure you are okay. I will give more of myself to you in the hopes of obtaining your love." This is usually at the expense of what is of the highest for both people. Co-dependency forms a tight knot and keeps both partners from growing and experiencing life within and beyond the relationship. At a subconscious level, both people agree to "play small" and remain insular. This suffocating care of the other to the exclusion of self is not love. There is no free-flowing and open dance in such a relationship. There is only inhibition, fear of expansion and change, and dullness, which is anything but love. In such a relationship, there is less chance for personal growth and little room for spiritual growth. When we stay in such small relationships, we often think we are doing so for the sake of the other whom we believe could not function without us. In most situations, this is a false belief. We are fooling ourselves, and we are depriving the other of the space and the chance to encounter the kind of inner conflict that allows for self-growth.

However, when one person in a relationship chooses to make him or herself unavailable to grow, the other can work on him or herself alone. An important goal is to learn to stand strong, clear, and unafraid within ourselves, to know the truth of who we are, and to be able to give, hold, and receive love just as it is in the moment—free of expectations and putting no restrictions on our loving. When we can hold ourselves in our wholeness no matter what is happening on the outside and within our relationships, we have truly come home to our spiritual selves. Then we are free. This means we have stepped far beyond our ego selves and the old ways to enter our true home in which sacredness becomes manifest in our daily lives. It also means that we have dissolved some karma between ourselves and the other person when we are free of the vagaries of a difficult relationship.

As in all parts of our lives, with increased consciousness, our wounding becomes the medium that propels us into healing. When our self-healing is in place, we can see all others beyond what we once saw as their limitations and instead see right into the sacred spaces of their goodness and their souls. When we choose to bring deep honor and Divine consciousness into our relationships, we are dancing with the other in the yoga of relationship. Within the yoga of relationship is where we find unconditional love. Such love has been in short supply for most people. However, as we commit ourselves to the path of conscious self-love, we can offer this unconditional love to all others. We are once again finding a way to replenish the well. Once this awakening into unconditional love occurs, we bring more freedom and lightness of being, more fun, and joy into all our relationships and the larger world. And our world changes for the better.

The list below brings some specific ideas we can use to change patterns in relationships that seem destructive.

*

During an argument, one or the other can call a time out with an intention to revisit the issue once emotions are not as strong. During this break, take time to reflect, write in your journal, repeat your mantra, walk, or move to release the tensions you have been carrying.

*

Always we can have the intention that we will commit to finding solutions to our differences. This may mean writing letters to each other, speaking from the heart, speaking from the place of "I" rather than blaming, and talking about "You." We can refuse to judge or blame; rather we will take full responsibility for our feelings and our words.

*

One powerful exercise is to reflect on what the other has said and then ask if your understanding is correct. Listening in this way means putting your agenda on hold until you have fully heard and understood the other. Once this reflection is clear, ask the other that your concerns be heard in similar ways. Reflecting on the other's words is key to decreasing misunderstandings and often provides a deeper understanding of your partner's thoughts, feelings, and wounding. Towards the end of such a conversation, each person can restate the most relevant thing that s/he heard the partner say. The second part of this exercise is to succinctly state again what she or he would like the partner to understand. Then, each person can state what she or he will do differently to avoid such problems in the future.

*

End such conversations by holding hands, breathing together, and looking into each other's eyes without speech until mutual loving flows once again.

*

Practice *The Eyes of the Soul* meditation with each other and share your experiences afterward. (See page 230 for the link to the recording.)

*

Tell your partner why she or he is special to you and why you love her or him.

209

*

Practice ending each day in loving ways and with gratitude for the other.

~~~~

This is love, as I know it today:

Love is a communion, a uniting with the other and with many others.

It is a mirroring of the other, reflecting the pain and the goodness of the other, the brokenness and soulfulness and the potentials.

Love is affirming.

It is joyous.

It is truth-speaking.

Love means working on oneself to become clear of negative karma and patterning.

Love means holding a clear, centered space for our partners and for those who are precious in our lives.

Love holds open doors for our partner to grow, to experience independence, and separation, as well as togetherness.

Love opens doors for each person's spiritual growth.

Love is kind and gentle. It also holds the ability to be strong when standing up for righteousness and one's own integrity.

Love holds the qualities of compassion and empathy.

Love is transformative, inspired, creative, and free.

Love is ever-changing, deepening and expanding. It becomes inclusive of the angels and the Divine in all Her aspects.

Flow, ease, and understanding of the other are all parts of our loving communication.

Love expressed in its fullness fosters healing for both you and your partner.

As our love expands, it reaches far and wide into our communities and into specific services we offer to others. In this way, we have our unique part in the healing of our world.

As our love expands even further, we embrace all others in the world and the Earth Herself. We become more humble, more ready to help and serve, and know that we are offering the best of ourselves for the sake of our communities and our world.

There are never-ending possibilities to all acts of love. Love can surprise us with unexpected gifts and sometimes miracles. We find love in the everyday moments with another and in the beauty and truth of loving words that we send or receive. Our deep and soulful loving contains the capacities to love all our brothers and sisters and all beings throughout the world and to do whatever is right and dharmic to serve others. Each time we let go, ask, and receive, we are in the presence of the Divine. This is love.

CONTEMPLATION

Write about your relationships:
    What positive karma is present?

    What difficult karma is present?

    What karma are you resolving?

If you are in a co-dependent relationship, write about it. What do you need to do differently for the well-being of both you and your partner?

Write about your loving ways:
    Your wholeness

    Your capacity for intimacy

    Your compassion and empathy.

What are your next steps to move further in loving ways?

CHAPTER 27

THE PRACTICE OF FORGIVENESS

When someone hurts us, we face several choices in our response. We may hold onto a sense of being wounded for a short time or a longer one. We can choose to withdraw into ourselves, thus keeping negative dynamics in place. We may withhold our forgiveness, which creates blockages within us. Or, because of the nature of the wounding, we may need to move away from this person. When it is advantageous to work through a problem, it is wise and healing to do so. Holding harmful dynamics in place causes a tear in the fabric of the relationship and of the universe. It keeps us from remembering that we all belong to one another. When we hang onto a sense of victimization, we cannot heal. Our emotional and physical health may suffer, sometimes in serious ways. This keeps us limited, angry, obsessive, depressed, and in states of victimhood.

Another approach that may seem more difficult is to commit to doing the inner work necessary to soften into a state of forgiveness. True forgiveness of another is often an arduous journey from states of feeling violated, angry, and betrayed to moving beyond our wounding into acceptance, understanding, compassion, and peace. To forgive means that we have come far enough in our contemplations to be able to witness another's actions from a much-expanded perspective. In true forgiveness, we enter a state of grace regarding the other. By doing so, we have resolved karma between the other and ourselves.

Some people seem to forgive easily and naturally. For most of us, however, forgiving another for harm done to us is not a quick or simple process. It usually takes place over time. Sometimes it takes years, and it may take lifetimes due to the karmic nature of disagreements and wounding. Just knowing that forgiveness is often a lengthy process can help us with the practice of forgiving another. At times in our society, we believe that we must forgive, especially as this is what we often hear from our religions. While this is karmically true, if we forgive too quickly, and because we think we must, there are often untoward consequences. We may suppress our anger and other difficult emotions. Then we "play nice" and continue to suffer due to the lack of true resolution. This way can take us only so far. Later, we may want (and need) to revisit this process of forgiveness more than once. It is only by forgiving from both our minds and our hearts that we can experience wholeness within ourselves.

Forgiveness has many permutations depending on the degree of harm and the willingness of the other to participate in the process of learning, communicating, and making amends. When one person is not able to be involved in the process, the work of forgiveness falls upon the other alone. It takes courage and soul searching, and often assistance from a skilled therapist for healing to take place so that we can come to a higher understanding and move forward with our lives. If we stay caught in self-righteousness and judgment of the other, we remain in ego states that keep us stuck and unable to see beyond the present suffering. As we do the contemplative work of forgiving, we uncover layers of pain, distortions, and sadness to the point of grief. Eventually, we find that there is so much more to the story for both the other person and for ourselves.

Along the path of forgiveness, we may remember ways in which we made relationship mistakes. In some instances, we may notice we are still carrying a variety of negative emotions about those situations, such as shame, fear, or guilt. Therefore, when we look at forgiveness in a relationship, we often open doorways into inner work that uncovers our own faults as well as those of the other person. Ultimately, such processing holds deep karmic clearing. When we can expand our vision and understanding, we know at the deepest levels of our being that we both exist as parts of the one fabric of Divine Consciousness. In this enlightened realm, there is no separation. There is only love at the level of our souls. Within this realm of recovery and loving-kindness, we all become teachers for one another. We come together to help each other heal. As long as we hold the wounding in our minds and heart, and if we continue to have anger towards the other, we are bound to that person and unable to move forward.

To forgive does not mean to forget. We cannot completely erase from our mind any traumatic event and we will hold the other person accountable for what he or she had done. If this accountability is not there, we will have to find a way to separate ourselves from the other. Along the way, no matter what happens with the other person, we can learn a lot about ourselves and others. Each such situation is worthy of contemplation over time. I find that an important goal is to evolve into a state of equanimity and grace regarding the other. When this occurs, we have resolved some important karma regarding another.

Deep forgiveness comes once we can see with expanded vision who the other is and why she or he would act as she had. This seeing is vastly different from our previous ego states. When this happens, through whatever work we have done within ourselves, we can step into the other person's shoes. Then we can see this person's wounding and brokenness, the attempts to overcome the pain by controlling his or her life, and by acting in exactly the ways that led to the original problems.

In an ideal situation, the other person in the relationship will participate in the process of forgiveness and there will be a dialogue between two people talking about how each felt wronged in the situation. Each person will express both feelings and needs and will take responsibility for his or her part in what has happened. These communications are often emotional, difficult, and draining; however, they are well worth the effort as they open doors to necessary change.

Once we can see all of this, our understanding becomes strong and clear. We will have compassion and we will realize that we are now acting from a position of neutrality and strength.

After both people have shared their fear, anger, and pain and have felt heard by the other, it is time for heartfelt apologies. A true, heartfelt apology will lead to a sense of relief and freedom on the part of the person apologizing. A true apology will include heartfelt remorse. Then ideally, both people will state how they will do things differently in the future. Following this, the work of the relationship is to hold to these commitments. Both people have inner work to understand the antecedents of the behaviors that led to this situation. A part of this work will be to make amends and to

215

practice living and communicating in new ways. This, then, is true forgiveness.

Sometimes, however, there are extenuating circumstances that make the act of forgiveness more complicated although still not impossible. True forgiveness can happen even if the other is unavailable to participate due to psychological distortions, unwillingness, or inability. It can happen with someone who has died. This is true because the energy of true forgiveness happens at the soul level, from one soul to another. Meditating on the situation between you and the other, praying for guidance and support with your process are ways to enter the path of forgiveness. We also can speak to the other energetically by imagining this person in front of us and talking directly to him or her. We can write letters that we burn instead of sending. Often it is important to get help in a therapist's office to do this sometimes-difficult work.

When we begin to understand all relationships and especially the difficult ones from a karmic perspective, we also attain a larger, expanded vision of our own wounding as well as others. We may also see that our current situations are the outgrowth of karma from other lifetimes that have come to the fore at this time for healing. We access this information with the help of therapists and healers who have a far-reaching vision. Meditation experiences can also catapult us into enlightened states and deep wisdom. Once these transformations occur, we free ourselves from previous beliefs that have kept us stuck. In this way, forgiveness happens naturally. The karmic dynamics that we, and/or our families have carried through generations are also resolved. There is immense freedom in this, and we are never the same.

When we follow the process of forgiveness, we usually experience great relief and a lightness of being. When the original love, whatever its nature, reignites and both people connect at deeper levels, we know that some karma is resolved. This is the yogic dance of forgiveness in its highest form.

CONTEMPLATION

Write about times in which you have forgiven others and what happened as a result.

Are there people you still want to forgive?

If so, how will you go about doing so?

Do you need help along the way? If so, what are the next steps you will take?

FORGIVENESS MEDITATIONS

When we practice forgiveness, we can move energies from those of judgment, rigidity, angst, and victimization to those of clarifying and understanding from a spiritual perspective. The first meditation is one in which you forgive another. This meditation can be practiced with any other person, currently in your life or no longer available. You will be seeing the essence of this person in these meditations and you will be shifting energies between the two of you. If you have been traumatized by another, it is best to do this meditation, and other healing work, in a therapist's office, as there may be other aspects of this release that require compassionate help from a professional.

The second Forgiveness Meditation is one in which you ask the other to forgive you. Often, we do not have the luxury of meeting with another; however, because we are energetic beings connected to one another, we can practice such a meditation and shift both the energies within and between the other and us.

You may need additional time at certain points in these meditations. Please pause the recording at any point along the way to contemplate all that needs expression. Then, resume the recording when you are ready to move forward.

You may want to practice these meditations with different people in your current life and from your past. The object, of course, is always to deepen healing.

I ASK FOR YOUR FORGIVENESS MEDITATION

This Forgiveness Meditation is one in which you ask the other to forgive you. Please practice this meditation to shift both the energies within and between yourself and another you have wronged.

You may want to use this meditation with different people in your current life and from your past. The object, of course, is always to deepen healing for yourself and others.

To listen to this meditation, use the QR Code below to go to this website: www.everydaysouldances.com/meditations.

I FORGIVE YOU MEDITATION

This meditation allows us to connect with healing energies and then extend them beyond ourselves to the other to help with shifts in perspective. Before you begin, please contemplate the following questions:

Whom do I need to forgive?

How ready am I to let the past problems go to enter a freer and more openhearted state?

You will find the recording of this meditation through the QR code below. It links you to www.everydaysouldances.com/meditations.

CONTEMPLATION

Write about your experience with these meditations.

What has been resolved?

Is there anything else that you need to do in terms of forgiveness of self or another?

What changes do you notice after experiencing these Forgiveness meditations?

CHAPTER 28

MOVING FROM HERE TO THERE IN RELATIONSHIP

Now that we have explored some of the complexities of relationships, we will pay attention to the qualities of healthy, loving ones. Many of these qualities are the same spiritual qualities that we focused on previously in these pages. This is not surprising since relationship is one of the great paths to the discovery of the Divine within us and the Divine within those we love.

From a spiritual perspective, we come into a relationship for two main purposes: to clear karma that only can be cleared through being in a relationship and to learn to love in better and deeper ways through our relationships with one another. First, we practice self-recovery and self-discovery so that we bring the best of ourselves into our partnerships. This is the gift we give of ourselves to offer to the other. When we can hold ourselves in a relationship with our wholeness and strength in place, we are dancing our unique soul dances in our relationships. When we can do this, we know that we have released negative karma and are manifesting our sacredness daily.

We consecrate ourselves to the other and promise to be constant in our loving, as best we can, through the vagaries of our lives. A part of our commitment is to truthfulness, openness in communication, and a willingness to tackle life's challenges together and over time. Implicit within the partnership is an openness to growing together as well as individually. A part of this growth deepens intimacy, sexuality, and emotional connectedness. As we practice these new ways, we grow beyond fear. We also will quest beyond the status quo to keep the relationship vibrant. We will learn to forgive ourselves and the other. This is the practice of having courage in a relationship, the courage to speak the truth, the courage to expect equality, the courage to confront problems in gentle, yet strong and clear ways, and the courage to move beyond stuck places.

In a healthy relationship, we lessen our need to control or judge the other or the situations in which we find ourselves. Instead, we are open to working together to find better ways to understand each other—learning when to compromise, when to yield, and when to stand firm. If this accountability is not there, we will have to find a way to separate ourselves from the other. Because we love the other, we commit to growing ourselves in the relationship and ask the other to grow along with us. This kind of growth takes time. Along the way, in good times and difficult ones, it is important to reflect on the growth of the relationship, on your own or in conversation together. Here are some helpful questions to consider:

"What am I learning about myself and the other in this relationship?"

"What can I do differently to solve relationship problems in kinder and wiser ways?"

"How do I take care of myself and my partner when _____ is happening?"

In answering these questions, you may find that you and your partner's commitment to developing positive communication patterns has allowed both of you to move forward with greater compassion. You may also find that you have reached an impasse that requires you to seek help. This is not an indication of failure. As we grow in compassion, we become more aware of any signs of past wounding in our partner. And we know through our own contemplations and psychological growth that wounding can be deep. As we grow in empathy, we become more sensitive to his or her needs for healing. Our partner's ways to accomplish this may be different from ours. Now, we are more able to honor and support that growth no matter what form it takes. At the same time, if we have trauma to heal, we will consciously dedicate ourselves to heal ourselves to bring our best to the table of relationship.

Unconditional and compassionate loving between partners leads to greater intimacy in any relationship as it inspires daily conversations, better problem-solving, and deepening experiences of sexuality. When we live in partnership with spiritual principles in place, we love deeply and well no matter what is happening around us. Another sign of spiritual health in a relationship is the ability to be grateful and humble in the face of such astonishing love. These soulful ways allow us to yield and open; thus, our love deepens.

One of the most beautiful aspects of growing spiritually in a relationship is that we experience the essence of God and Goddess within our partner and ourselves. In each day, in each action, and each word, we have opportunities to create sacred union and kinship. We have been made for this. Every time we speak and act from a conscious and lighted place towards our partner, we walk farther on our sacred paths, clearing old karma from times in which our words and actions were not so kind and gentle—in past lives, in previous relationships, or from any debilitating dynamics within our families of origin in this life. This is the yoga of relationship.

As we practice conscious compassion, we experience a deep and abiding love that grows stronger and truer over time. We realize that we are serving the Divine through our choices with our partner and that we are growing in Divinity within ourselves. This, too, is the yoga of relationship.

Elaine Hoem

CONTEMPLATION

Name the ways in which you love well. Honor yourself for doing so.

Write about those areas in which you can make improvements:

Clarity and kindness in communication

Listening well

Addressing difficult emotions
Your own

Your partner's

Playing and having fun

Sensual and sexual expression

What changes would you like to make?

What help do you need along the way?

CHAPTER 29

QUALITIES OF A LOVING RELATIONSHIP

As time passes and your relationship becomes healthier through the positive steps you each are taking, a new question arises: "How do we make positive shifts in our relationships from where we are today in our love for one another that will lead us to the actual experience of unconditional love?"

The answers to that question come moment-by-moment and day-by-day and every answer is unique to each of us. Putting them into practice takes time, as do the changes that will happen as a result. How we attain them is distinctive to each of us. The more we remember and pay attention, the easier these changes become. Like any other habitual pattern, we want to shift, we do so gradually—one step at a time. This means making one shift in communicating and loving and then practicing it repeatedly until this change becomes the new habit.

The following suggestions are ideas that are rich in possibilities for growth and loving change. They are well worth remembering and practicing daily. Even seemingly small changes can have profound effects. Please feel free to add to this list through your own knowledge, wisdom, and experiences.

* Choose not to react in anger, and, instead, take some time to breathe, to write, and to reflect. Then consider your words and intentions carefully before you speak about a problematic issue.

* Choose to overlook your partner's habits that previously drove you crazy.

* Take responsibility for your part of a problem instead of blaming the other.

* Tell your partner what you need.

- Ask your partner what he or she needs and really listen to what is being said.

- Commit to working through the difficult parts in your relationship with your partner or by yourself.

- Ask your partner to join you in exploring new ideas about how to bring more lightness and fun and deeper loving into your relationship.

- Encourage your partner to explore other parts of his or her being to grow.

- At times, step back so that your partner may step forward into greater wholeness.

- Say "I love you and this is why: _____" (be specific).

- Ask "How can I help?"

- Find creative new ways to grow in relationship—in communication, in spiritually, sexuality, and sensuality.

- Ask for help when you are stuck.

- Look into your partner's eyes long enough to find all the feelings your beloved is holding.

- Tell your partner "Thanks for being _____" and "Thank you for being you."

- Step forward and speak out if you have been too passive.

- Live in calm rather than harried ways.

- Bow in NAMASTE to the person whom you love.

- Many of these ideas can apply to any relationship—our co-workers, our children, our parents, and our friends. They can inform how we act, love, and speak when in any community setting.

- You may have other ideas that would be good to write about and to share.

CONTEMPLATION

Write about your successes in loving.

Write about your challenges in loving.

What are the next steps for you to take to love better?

EYES OF THE SOUL MEDITATION

This meditation is a partnership meditation. It is effective for deepening your knowledge of each other by seeing through the eyes of the soul into the soulfulness of the other.

Practice this meditation with a partner, especially one whom you would like to know better. Use this recording to stay better focused on your partner and your joint experiences.

You will find the recording for the meditation through the QR code below. It links you to www.everydaysouldances.com/meditations.

CONTEMPLATION

What are your thoughts and ideas about enhancing your loving ways?

What is your experience of this meditation? How will it help to move you even more deeply into understanding and loving?

Talk with your partner about your experiences with this meditation.

How will you keep these intimate and soulful connections in place?

PART VII

YOU WILL FIND ME EVERYWHERE

CHAPTER 30

THE INFINITE EMBRACE

The love of the Divine Feminine always holds us in an infinite embrace. We only need to open to Her to find Her everywhere. We find Her in nature and the present moment. We always find Her when we open to our love flowing within and when our love flows outwards towards others and in service to others. Her energy, the energy that fuels our entire universe, is within and without eternally.

We may experience our relationship with Her as something that has been with us forever, or as something that we have been searching for that always seems just out of reach. Know that our communion with Her can be realized in an instant. It is the result of a longing to consecrate our lives in the search for wholeness. At times, She comes to us in surprising and unexpected ways. We find Her in our meditations, in the conscious use of our breath, in our prayers, in our psychological and spiritual growth, in our contemplations, our dances, and in centering our attention on Her in our daily lives.

She is everywhere and within everyone and everything. Her energies, those energies that fuel our entire universe are within and without eternally. It is in the sacred space of deeply listening to a friend, a loved one, a child, or even a member of our community whose ways differ from ours. She is present when we make love. With Her in our hearts, our lovemaking becomes sacred, and our ecstasy knows no bounds. When we call to Her, we are automatically opening to the potentiality of our highest Selves. We also are opening gateways to the saints, the angels, and other ascended beings who are available to support us when we ask. She resides within the wise words of a friend or stranger, the wise and funny things that others say, a stunning moment with an exquisite blossom, and when the sun turns the river to gold.

In our knowing that this is so, we gradually become empty of ego, of desires, and of worn-out ways that no longer serve. In this emptying, we become open to receiving It All. There is no doubt when this happens. This is a love greater than we can imagine and yet, it is exactly right, perhaps for the first time.

We can call on Her at any moment—in gratitude, in crisis, when we need help, and when others do. She pays attention when we are scared, depressed, or anxious. She sees more clearly than we do the terror, pain, degradation, and destruction that are happening in our world. She also knows well the beauty, magnificence, and all the infinite possibilities of that same world. She contains it all and helps us to do so as well. All we need to do is ask. This is a two-way communion—from Her to you and from you to Her. These energies flow both ways if we pay attention. Remember that this is so.

She resides in your golden heart. Your heart is a temple for Her. It is a lighted place, as exquisite and beautiful as you would like to envision it. There is no separation. Whenever we open to this awareness and depth, our hearts unlock and becomes brilliant and overflowing with love, thanksgiving, humility, and with Her grace. Others may notice, be touched, and potentially changed just by your presence alone.

She resides in your tears, your heartaches, fears, and deep grief. She resides in your creativity, your enthusiasm, in your laughter, and all your loving ways. When you speak your highest truths in a clear, strong, and gentle voice, it is Her voice speaking through you. When you speak out for justice and righteousness for all people, your words carry forth Her voice. She moves through you into your everyday actions. This is how we create sacred ways in our daily lives. This is love and this is grace.

When you serve others, you are Her hands. When you listen and understand with compassion, you are Her ears and Her compassionate heart. When you walk on this earth, you are walking on Her sacred ground. When you create beautiful music and words in soul-filled ways, Her songs and Her voice ring out throughout the world. Her love carries forth when you touch another with gentleness and softness. When you live a consecrated life, your sacred soul dances become Her dances. We are here on this earth to express Goddess consciousness in all our daily acts.

This is how we each do our part to enliven our existence and to help in the uplifting growth of our communities and our beautiful planet. When we burst forth with the glorious energies of our love, we carry others with us as well. Each such act more than counterbalances those acts of lesser consciousness. As Soul Dancers, we become light bearers—loving and radiant beings who illuminate the way, a gift so needed in our world today.

Do not doubt the significance of your importance in this cosmic tapestry. Your pure energies radiate out from you into the universe. On the spiritual path, we live out Her energies and express them in the most magnificent ways possible. When we choose wisely, we bring forth Her gifts. Each time we do so, what we create is amazing, wondrous, and healing for all of us.

There are thousands of ways to consciously experience our connection with Her. Remember that She resides within and without, closer to you than your breath. Simply open to all possible ways of knowing that presence. Often a simple shift in awareness is all that it takes to find that connection, no matter what we are doing. We may be doing the dishes and wanting to just to get them done. Alternatively, we can do the dishes while remembering our Divinity and our Oneness with All That Is. Then we enter a state of pure light while performing a simple, everyday task. Women may find Her in certain ways. Men will find Her in other ways unique to them. All of us can bring Her forward into our lives and our loving. This is grace. This is love manifesting in myriad forms through us, around us, and for us.

Trust in the ways that are uniquely yours to find All That Is in all Its numinous wonder.

CHAPTER 31

AHAM PREMA "I AM DIVINE LOVE"

AHAM PREMA is a mantra from the Kashmir Shaivism tradition. In English, it translates to I AM DIVINE LOVE. It is like the HAMSA mantra – I AM THAT. This mantra brings us to experiences of universal consciousness, the transcendental state that we have been moving towards. It deepens our experience of Oneness with All That Is.

Its purpose is to increase our experience of the Divine Light of the Mother that dwells within. As we increasingly live in this state, we are a conduit for these energies to flow out from us to others in our world and beyond. It is a form of blessing for all of us to bring more love into the world.

You can practice this mantra at any time. It is good to do so especially when you or another is worried, fearful, or falling back into lesser states.

Here are some beginning ideas for the use of this mantra. I like to practice it by internally repeating AHAM on the inhalation, and PREMA, on the exhalation until you establish a rhythm between your prana (life force energy) and the mantra. Once you have this rhythm in place, you can contemplate all the ways that you are Divine Love at any moment in time.

For example:

AHAM PREMA (I Am Divine Love) as I enter the silence.

AHAM PREMA (I Am Divine Love) as I practice loving and caring for myself.

AHAM PREMA (I Am Divine Love) as I send blessings out to the others I encounter today.

AHAM PREMA (I Am Divine Love) as I remember to have deep gratitude for all that is given in my life.

AHAM PREMA (I Am Divine Love) when I listen to another with compassion.

AHAM PREMA (I Am Divine Love) when I care for my family.

AHAM PREMA (I Am Divine Love) when I serve others in my community and the world.

AHAM PREMA (I Am Divine Love) as I broaden my vision and my intentions for my life.

AHAM PREMA (I Am Divine Love) when I pray.

AHAM PREMA (I Am Divine Love) when I love.

AHAM PREMA (I Am Divine Love) as I walk gently upon our Mother Earth.

Feel free to add more ways as you repeat this mantra. Remember that every time you live with consciousness, you are practicing AHAM PREMA. It is a centering prayer, a remembrance, and a stabilizing, unifying, and peace-building communion with Her.

I AM SHE; SHE IS ME MEDITATION

This meditation contains imagery to bring all our ways into a place of wholeness so that it is easier for us to access the truth of who we are as a sacred being in communion with the Mother, the Luminous One.

Please follow the QR code below to link to this website: www.everydaysouldances.com/meditations.

Elaine Hoem

CONTEMPLATION

Write about your communion with the Divine Feminine.

How does this communion expand and deepen your sense of Self?

Write a prayer to Her now that you know Her better. Include what is most important to you. Then listen....

Revisit prayers to Her often.

CHAPTER 32

DANCING YOUR SACRED DANCES

It is time to put all this together. I hope that you, Dear One, have been moved by the words and ways of this book. I honor all that you have accomplished along the way to learn, to grow, to transform, to relinquish old beliefs, and to embrace new ways. Each time we are prayerful, each time we act with intention and attention, and each time we are in communion with another, we are dancing That Which Is Sacred as She moves through us. As we make all our ways sacred, the steps of our dances consecrate all the movements of our daily life. Practice your Everyday Soul Dances when you are shopping, when you are listening to another, when you are writing in your journal, and when you dream strong dreams that show the way. Even as I write these words, I see vast possibilities as the *Everyday Soul Dance* readers practice these ways. In doing so, we are bettering our world and ourselves. We are richer in our loving and we are showing others the way home to their most loving selves.

I trust that, at this point, you are already delighting in new ways of being, that you are more relaxed, clearer in your visions, more open in your loving, and more united to the One who resides within. With continued consciousness and practice, we all will be moving forward, spiraling home in enlightened ways, and embracing All That Is within and without.

This is a journey, a journey of your soul. It is never-ending, infinite, expansive, and amazing beyond belief. Insights may arise at any moment. These insights can create openings that change everything—your perspective, your beliefs about yourself, and how you move through your world, to name just a few. Everything and anything can add color, creativity, and expression to your soul's dance.

As you commit to walking this golden path, the steps along the way become clear and more obvious—an intuition here, a message from another that sparks a light within, a touch that opens you to unexpressed emotion, an awe-inspired view of the sunset on the snow on the mountain peaks. Any experience that softens you and opens your heart will be another message from Her. When we remember Her and then remember who we are in our greatest expression of our Self, we become still and empty. In this emptiness, our defenses release, and our boundaries disappear. Then we are replete with Her presence, filled beyond imagining with Her, Her love, Her grace, Her wisdom, and Her creativity.

May you move through your life in enlightened, graceful, and grace-filled ways, always remembering to bless yourself as you return to Her. May you be creative, honest, and clear in all your loving ways. May you bow down in humility to the wonder of it all along the way. May all your ways be filled with grace, always.

In a dream, I am with a group of people in their compound in a misty forest setting. It is the middle of the night… quiet, languid, and peaceful. We are silently performing tasks within the rooms. One room has beautiful indigenous artwork and shelves of books. This room is small, filled with beauty, knowledge, and serenity.

Now I am with another, a sacred partner for this time and place. I am at peace here. I have a deep sense of belonging and rightness. This is exactly where I am to be and who I am to be just now. Everything is in slow motion. There are others in these rooms carrying out similar tasks. In this quiet dark night, we are connected to one another, and to the Goddess in one of her Native forms. This is a time of communion, of fullness, of stillness. We are enveloped into the sacred ways of the Mother. We each are living our greatest, yet simple, everyday dances and doing so through everyday tasks.

There is no sense of urgency. There is only the night, the movements, the fluidity, and the sanctity. Every movement, every task, every look, and every feeling is a part of this dance. Everything is sacred. All is holy and sated with love. This everyday soul dance moves us deeper into the center of All That Is, into cosmic grace.

This is a Soul Dance that is both ancient and new, all-embracing, and replete with Her grace-filled energies. I feel gratitude and enter this communion. I am powerful in this knowing, clear, connected, and still.

Each time I revisit this dream, I breathe deeply and ease back into this way of being in which I am both empty and filled with the sacred. I remember and practice such ways as I go about my daily life. In doing so, I honor my potential, my higher Self, and my being at one with the Sacred Feminine as I remember that She infuses my everyday ways.

The Everyday Soul Dances exist when we bring consciousness to all our acts. The gifts we receive can be found in the presence of the Goddess' spiritual qualities coming forth in our daily lives. This is a way of the Feminine Spirit. This is grace. Once we touch these places, we know at a deep level that all life is infinitely precious, even in the hardest of times. We know that we have only this moment, however, it manifests. When we remember and pay attention, we bow with humility and honor our lives as our daily sacred dance.

CHAPTER 33

I AM THAT I AM

I Am That I Am,
Present here on this Earth,
Living, breathing, learning, and finding my freedom.

I am my lineage,
My pain and my joy
My past and my future,
And the goodness and greatness of all that have gone before me.

And I am more.
I am the breath and the silence that draws me
Into the cave of my heart, and the spirit of love,
And the knowledge that I Am at one with the Goddess.

In this knowing, I know there is no difference between Her and me.

We are.
We are a part of All That Is.
We are not separate from the birds, the fish, the flowers,
The waters, the snow
The desert, the mountains, and trees,
The deer, the algae
The sun, moon, and stars.

We are caretakers of the living, pulsating being
That is this Earth and all its creatures,
And we are here for Her healing.

And we are more.
When we enter the silence and into the light,
We touch the worlds of the angels
And otherworldly guides
Who hold us in their hands and their love,
And who give us the strength of the mountains,
The knowledge of our greatness,
The knowing of our place in the grand scheme of the Goddess,
The courage to act upon our wisdom,
And the grace to be strong and gentle
In all that we do.

Then we are one with
The Goddess,
Our guides and the angels.

We are.
We are Beauty.
We are Joy.
We are One.
We are.
HAMSA.

CONTEMPLATION

What are some examples of your Everyday Soul Dances?

What happens when you remember that you are an ecstatic being connected to the Divine?

How will you maintain and honor these energies so that they become more pervasive in your daily life?

CHAPTER 34

A CLOSING FOR NOW

We are coming to the final words of this book—and at the same time, we open to continuing these ways filled with new possibilities. I hope you have experienced expansion simply by reading and thinking about the possibilities for peace and a loving life expressed on these pages. I trust that you have grown in awareness of your Self and your Spirit and the existence of those in others and that if you have begun the practices that I have shared here, you are already finding more joy, more connection, and more love.

We are all brilliantly lit stars shining in the fields of Divine Consciousness. We have been together in these fields many times before, for we are One Consciousness of infinite possibilities and astonishing beauty. Our souls light the way. We have known the graceful steps of the Everyday Soul Dances through all times and we have danced them together throughout eternity. We have danced them with the pantheon of the Gods and Goddesses, and with all people, all places, and all experiences. Together, they illuminate our fullness, our richness, and the ways to our true home. The direction we must take is in the message of a stranger, in the embrace of a beloved, and the words shared here. They teach us how to deepen into sacred understanding. We choose these experiences when we feel our brokenness and pain, when we allow ourselves to be encircled by the grace-filled arms of the Mother, the saints, angels, and ascended masters, and when we are healed. Our mantras, prayers, and loving gestures divinely inspire us to keep following these dances. We have faith that we will dance with many partners along the way who will share in our growth and joy. Each such union is a gift and a blessing that we carry with us forever.

When we put all this together, our practices become vibrantly colored threads that we weave into the tapestry of our soul dancing life. Your tapestry and your ways are unique, inimitable, beautiful, and filled with all the brilliance of your wholeness, wonder, and joy.

As you live your sacred ways each day you will be touching others who are also moving through their lives, sometimes in difficult ways, and in miraculous ones. Do not doubt the possibilities and the wonder of what you are creating as your life intersects with theirs. The cosmic stage upon which you are dancing contains delicious surprises beyond anything you could have imagined on your own. This is so because you are embodying the Goddess, the Divine Mother, the Sacred Feminine. Every time you pay attention to the sacred, you are doing Her dance, and it is always a magnificent one.

Consecration, constancy, courage, and contemplation are the principles that will bring you home to those places within yourself that are most vital and dear to you. Choose any practice that calls to you and then practice and play with its ways that bring you joy, forward movement, and expansiveness. Remember to commit to practice for 90 days until it becomes a part of your life. Add other practices as you can. Remember that Soul Dances are ways of living life rather than training to be completed in a specific length of time. I hope and trust that you will find more freedom and joy as you make inner and outer shifts.

Please continue to add the Soul Dance meditations that call to you. Each time you meditate your experience may be quite different. Remember that each time you meditate you are creating new neuropathways that become the threads of the beautiful tapestry that we constantly weave with the Mother.

In our dreams and new states of awareness, deep emotions may come forth to be expressed, even some that have been buried for many years or even lifetimes. When this happens, allow their expression, write, contemplate, and pray for guidance and release. When you cannot solve these deeper issues on your own, seek help from the wise ones in your life.

When we do our soulful dances long enough and completely enough, we soften and become gentler and more thoughtful. We become more sensitive to our partners and all those around us. Each day, and in each moment, we know that, in everything we do, there is only the dance.

You may find wise spiritual teachers or meditation groups to further your practices. As you explore different ways, trust your intuition as to which ones draw you forward in your spiritual search or not. You will know the rightness of such a fit when you feel uplifted, lighter, and more joyful. Such teachers offer service for the upliftment of humanity; they are not ego-bound in the least.

Practice remembering your beauty, your potential, your love, and your goodness. Reflect often on what you are experiencing and on how you are opening. Above all, be very gentle and loving with yourself every day. You will find that you are creating new ways that are uniquely yours. Share them with others. Bless it all. Honor it all.

Remember that She is always calling us to love in all situations, with all the people in our lives. She is asking us to take loving care of our Earth. Sometimes this love is fiery and tall. Sometimes it is as gentle as the caress we offer to an infant. This love sees deeply into the heart and soul of the other. It is sublime and real. All Her ways and all your ways make up your unique love story every day.

I wish you the absolute best and look forward to our being together again as you continue with your Everyday Soul Dances.

Dear One, Welcome Home.

CHAPTER 35

SHE SPEAKS

My Most Beautiful Dear One,

Thank you for your attention to these words and these ways, for your willingness to explore, and for opening to the truths of who you are. You have come far in this journey. I honor and celebrate you and invite you always to continue your lifelong sacred dances. Always remember that this journey home is all about love—love in its infinite forms, love expressed in large and small ways, love even when broken, and love expressed in your fullness.

By now, you know what brilliant and transcendent adventures your Soul dances encompass for you. They are grace-filled gifts without measure. All you must do is practice the ways, over and over, each day and every day, as best you can, paying attention to who you are each day, contemplating who you are to become, and dancing your sacred dances in stillness, simplicity, humility, love, gratitude, and honor.

Now you know some of the ways forward. I trust that you will continue to invent unique and beautiful steps of your own. Perhaps you will share them with others and watch how rich, expansive, and scintillating your world becomes.

Be steady in your ways. Deepen your communications with others. Celebrate your greatness, your goodness, and your endless possibilities as you move into new ways of being. Always bow to your inner Self and know that you are never alone. I Am your eternal companion. Honoring Who I Am within you provides astonishing fulfillment, a deeper knowing, a higher truth, and greater access to My light and grace. My purpose is to serve you and to awaken you so that you will know Me. Your purpose is to be My hands, My voice, and My expressions within your world.

Knowing Me is part of the Divine plan. First, you had to know separateness, pain, and sorrow beyond measure. These were your testing grounds as you fell into despair so that you would search for Me and then find Me within the radiance of your golden Heart, in your relations, and in All That Is. Now the possibilities are eternal, endless, and greater than you could possibly imagine. Do not limit your potential by doubt. You are worthy beyond measure.

May your wounds be healed at all levels of your being. May all your karmas be resolved. May your tears wash away your emptiness, fear, and lack of love. May you open to and delight in My myriad forms. May you deepen your connection to your sacred Self, to all others, to All That Is, and to Me, your Mother. May you love deeply and well.

Remember your beauty, your richness, your potential, your love, and your goodness. Remember your sacred Self, and always allow Me to guide your ways and all your days. Love well. Laugh often. Bow with humility, and open to grace, as you continually return home to your most precious and magnificent Self.

I am a bridge, a companion, and a guide. I am the light to show you the way. I Am your very essence, and you are my most sacred Self.

Remember that you are love and that you are loved. I thank you for accepting My deepest love, for hearing My words, and for your opening to Me eternally and forever.

NAMASTE

I honor the place in you,
In which the entire universe dwells.
It is a place of love, of light, of truth, and of peace.
When you are in that place in you
And I am in that place in me,
We are one.

ACKNOWLEDGEMENTS

Throughout the years, many people were teachers and guides for me in profound and healing ways. With them, I have grown, cried, laughed, released ancient karmas, and learned unconditional love. To each and all of you, I honor you and I am grateful. You know who you are. Many thanks to each one of you.

Over many years, I have followed a spiritual path based on ancient yogic traditions. This path is the backdrop for so much of this book. My interest in Transpersonal Psychology continues to expand and deepen through the beautiful practices of this tradition and the teachings of its leaders.

There are many others who I have met on retreats in Assisi, on Isla Mujeres and Tulum, Mexico, and on the island of Crete—women who opened themselves to the spiritual gifts of these experiences and to the soulful connections we had with one another.

Then some wonderful friends became early readers of this book. I am immensely humbled and grateful and so appreciative of your willingness to help bring the highest possible form to this book. These friends are Marta Adams, Rhonda Ashurst, Patti Davin, Chris DeGraff, Solomon Karmel, Joanna Pizur, and Arline Zeigler. Your ways, so similar and so different from mine, add strength, clarity, insight, and wisdom to my words. Your edits and recommendations brought more clarity and light to my original words.

I thank the staff at Balboa Press for taking my manuscript and turning it into a book that is published and sent out into the world for others to read. It takes a group of others to bring a book to fruition and Balboa Press provided exactly this team to do so. What an amazing process to turn the manuscript over to you and have it come back to me complete in book form.

Rosie Pearson is the editor of this book. Rosie, you became dear to me during this process, and you were brilliant and wise in your editing. You seamlessly entered my mind, heart, and vision for *Everyday Soul Dances* to bring my words into a more lustrous and harmonious whole. I have such joy and appreciation for your editing skills and gentle patience as I learned about editing along the way. In working with my words, you became more than an editor – a friend, a teacher, and a wise counselor. I am grateful.

And, last but not least, this book has become a collaborative family effort. I offer great thanks and appreciation to my three sons. I thank you, Don Conrad, for your brilliant cover design, website design, and for setting up 21st century technology for me. I also thank you for your easy patience with all my learning along the way. Many thanks to you, Bob Conrad, for all the recordings and their edits and your final proofreading of this book. I am in awe of both of you for your brilliant creativity and many talents. We have navigated wonderful possibilities, words, music, styles, and colors together. Your contributions to this book and my work bring great joy to me. As it has evolved, we have an amazing team as we worked together to bring this book to fruition.

I also thank my son, Keith Conrad, for always sending love my way and for giving me even more reason to get these words out in the world. This comes in the way of your children and the legacy we all must create a better world for such amazing young ones. You and your family bring to fruition in a very tangible way what it means to care for and love others to foster their greatest and highest growth.

FROM THE AUTHOR

If you have questions or would like to schedule Everyday Soul Dance coaching sessions with me, you can reach me by my contact information below.

I look forward to hearing from you.

If this book is of value to you, and you think it might be important for others in your life, please share it with your friends and family through social media, in person, and in other ways that you connect. You could invite me to a reading and Soul Dance experience at your book group or yoga class, or you could gather friends together for a Soul Dance experience. And please write a review. It can be just a few sentences written to your favorite bookseller's online page about *Everyday Soul Dances*. In doing so, you will be one of the networkers to spread the Everyday Soul Dance messages, one of the Soul Dancers. In this way, we will create a Soul Dance community that is worldwide and very much in keeping with the interconnections we are all making.

Please join my Facebook page— Everyday Soul Dances—and my email list: everydaysouldances@gmail.com. I will be adding new Soul Dances, contemplative practices, and meditations to this web page. Your voice and ways will also have a forum there. I hope that many readers will share your thoughtful ideas to help expand our visions of these ways on Facebook. Your words and insights will be much appreciated and, by doing so, you will assist in creating a Soul Dancer community along with me.

Many thanks,
Elaine

ABOUT THE AUTHOR

Elaine Hoem was a psychotherapist for nearly 50 years. She is a meditation teacher, a retreat leader, and a life coach. Elaine always has been fascinated with people, how they love and how they transform into more beautiful versions of themselves. In writing and publishing this book, she hopes to guide others as they deepen their spirituality and, in the process, enhance their lives.

Elaine currently lives in Reno, Nevada where she enjoys walks along the Truckee River, classical music, subline foods in the local restaurants, and time with friends and family.

CONTACT INFORMATION

Facebook: Everyday Soul Dances
Website: www.everydaysouldances.com
Email: everydaysouldances@gmail.com

ENDNOTES

1   Peter Hayes, "The Mystery of Karma Part 1: Sita's Ring," *Darshan Magazine #2 – Breakthrough*, (South Fallsburg, NY: SYDA Foundation, 1987), pp. 83-87; "The Mystery of Karma Part 2: The Curtain of Rebirth," *Darshan Magazine #3 - The Curtain of Rebirth*, 1987, pp. 61-65; "The Mystery of Karma: Conclusion: Beyond Destiny" *Darshan Magazine #6 - Meditation*, 1987, pp. 91-93.

2   Gary Zukav, *Seat of the Soul*, Chapters: Evolution and Karma. (New York: Fireside - Simon and Schuster, 1990), pp. 19-32 and pp 33-46.

3   Namdev Hayes, "The Mystery of Karma Part 4: Changing Our Destiny," *Darshan Magazine #5 - The Power of Discipleship*, 1987, pp. 93-96.

4   Hayes, "The Mystery of Karma Part 3: I.O.U," *Darshan Magazine #4 - The Path of Action*, 1987, pp. 64-67.

5   Eknath Easwaran, *Bhagavad-Gita*- 2nd ed., (Tomales, California: Nilgiri Press, 2007), pp. 99-103.

6   Swami Gitananda, "The Splendor of the Chakras," *Darshan Magazine #41-42 - Kundalini - The Awakening and the Unfolding*, 1990, pp. 31-39.

7   Barbara Brennan, *Hands of Light - A Guide to Healing Through the Human Energy Field* (New York: Bantam Books, Doubleday Dell Publishing Group, 1987), pp. 37-40.

8   Brennan, *Hands of Light*, inserts between pp. 44-45.

9   Mayo Clinic, www.mayoclinic.org/diseases-conditions/broken-heart-syndrome/symptoms-causes/syc-20354617.

10   Joseph Addison, *New England Primer*, The first appearance of this prayer dates to the 1784 edition of *The New England Primer*. This prayer can be found in many editions of books for children and adults since its first appearance.

RECOMMENDED READINGS

THE BODY

Candice Pert. Your Body Is Your Subconscious Mind. DVD. Boulder CO: Sounds True, 2002.
Phillips, Jan. *Divining the Body: Reclaim the Holiness of Your Physical Self.* Woodstock, VT: Skylight Path Publishing, 2005.

ENERGY HEALING

Brennan, Barbara, *Hands of Light.* Los Angeles: Bantam Books, 1987.
Emerging Light: A Journey of Personal Healing. New York: Bantam Books, 1993.

GODS AND GODDESSES

Bolen, Jean Shinoda. *Goddesses in Everywoman*, New York: Harper Collins, 1984; Quill (1ˢᵗ ed.), 2004.
Gods in Everyman. New York: Harper and Row, 1989.
Estes, Clarissa Pinkola. *Untie the Strong Woman: Blessed Mother's Immaculate Love for the Wild Soul.* Boulder: Sounds True, 2013.

HEALING

Bolen, Jean Shinoda Bolen. *Close to the Bone: Life-Threatening Illness and the Search for Meaning.* New York: Touchstone Books, Simon & Schuster, 2002.
Hay, Louise L. *You Can Heal Your Life.* Carlsbad, CA: Hay House, 1984.
Sha, Zhi Gang. *Soul Mind Body Medicine: A Complete Soul Healing System for Optimum Health and Vitality.* Novato, CA: New World Library, 2006.

JOURNALING

Cameron, Judith. *The Artist's Way: A Spiritual Path to Higher Creativity.* New York: Tarcher, Putnam Publishing Group, 1992.

PRAYER

Montano, Angela. *21 Days of Prayer to Change your Life.* www.dailyom.com.

PSYCHOTHERAPY

Gottlieb, Lori. *Maybe You Should Talk to Someone*. New York: Houghton Mifflin Harcourt Publisher, 2019.

RELATIONSHIP

Kassel, Charlotte. *If The Buddha Dated*. New York: Penguin Group, 1999.
Levine, Steven & Levine, Ondrea. *Embracing the Beloved: Relationship as a Path of Awakening*. New York: Doubleday, 1995.
O'Donohue, John. *To Bless The Space Between Us: A Book of Blessings*. New York: Doubleday, 2008.
Peck, M. Scott. *The Road Less Traveled: A New Psychology of Love*. Atlanta: Turner Publishing, 1992.
Squadra, John. *This Ecstasy*. Brooks, Maine: Hermes Press, 1996.
www.RelationshipRepairGame.com.

SACRED POETRY

Barks, Coleman. *A Year with Rumi*. New York: Harper Collins, 2006.
De Jong, Ana Lisa. *Seeking the Light: Poetry for the Soul*. New Zealand: Lang Book Publishing, 2016.
Knutson, Donna. *Finding God on Mayberry Street*. Omaha: Reverend Donna Ministries, 2017.

THE SOUL'S JOURNEY

Aurobindo, Shri. *The Psychic Being: Soul - Its Nature, Mission and Evolution*. Pondicherry, India: Sri Aurobindo Ashram, 1989.
Avari, Andrea. *A Hit of Heaven: A Soul's Journey through Illusion*. Nashville: Cold Tree Press, 2008.
Borysenko, Joan. *7 Paths to God: The Ways of the Mystic*. Carlsbad, CA: Hay House, 1997.
Easwaran, Eknath. *Bhagavad Gita* (2nd ed.). Tomales, CA: Nilgiri Press, 2007.
Harris, Maria. *Dance of the Spirit: The Seven Steps of Women's Spirituality*. New York: Bantam Books, 1989.
Kornfield, Jack. www.jackkornfield.com.
Kornfield, Jack & Feldman, Christina. *Soul Food*. San Francisco: Harper Collins, 1996.
Moore, Thomas. *Care of the Soul: A Guide for Cultivating Depth and Sacredness in Everyday Life*. New York: Harper Collins, 1992.

263

Remen, Rachel Naomi. *My Grandfather's Blessings*. New York: Riverhead Books, 2000.

Kitchen Table Wisdom: Stories That Heal. New York: Riverhead Books, 2006.

Wiederkehr, Macrina. *A Tree Full of Angels: Seeing the Holy in the Ordinary*. New York: Harper Collins, 1998.

Woodman, Marion and Mellick, Jill. *Coming Home to Myself: Reflections for Nurturing a Woman's Body and Soul*. San Francisco: Conari Press,1998.

Zukav, Gary. *Seat of the Soul*. New York: Simon & Schuster, 1990.

RESOURCES

ENERGY HEALERS

Black, Peggy. *Multidimensional Channel, Sound and Energy Worker*
www.morningmessages.com.
www.peggyblack.com.
Brady, Nancy. *Intuitive Guide* www.nancybrady.com.

MUSIC

Elcano, Philip. *RainDance* – RainDance CD. Background Music for Guided Meditations. Reno: Desert Productions, 1991.

Premal, Deva. *Mantras for Precarious Times*. CD. Boulder: White Swan Records, 2010.

Roth, Gabrielle. *Ecstatic Dance: The Gabrielle Roth Collection*. DVD. Louisville, CO: Sounds True Publishing, 2000.

Williamson, Chris. *The Changer and the Changed* - "Song of the Soul." CD. CD Baby at www.store.cdbaby.com, 2004 also available at www.chriswilliamson.com.

RETREATS

Davis, Bruce & Davis, Ruth. *Silent Stay Retreats*. www.silentstay.com.
Rosenberg, Karen. www.islawomensretreat.com. Facebook page: *Portals to the Self*.

SACRED MOVEMENT

David, Ruth. *Sacred Movement Ritual: At Home Meditation Course*. www.SilentStay.com

Printed in the United States
by Baker & Taylor Publisher Services